Horizons

Phonics and Reading

K

Teacher's Guide 2
Lessons 41–80

Author: Pollyann O'Brien, M.A.

Editor: Alan L. Christopherson, M.S.

Alpha Omega Publications, Inc. • Chandler, Arizona

Printed in the United States of America

ISBN 0-7403-0306-6

Scope & Sequence

Lesson 1

Letter **a**
- letter recognition
- short **a** sound
- recognizing and forming upper-case and lower-case **a**

Lesson 2

Letter **b**
- letter recognition
- beginning and ending letter **b** sound
- sound of **ba**
- recognizing and forming upper-case and lower-case **b**

Lesson 3

Letter **d**
- letter recognition
- letter **d** sound
- sound of **dă**
- recognizing and forming upper-case and lower-case **d**

Lesson 4

Letter **o**
- letter recognition
- beginning sound of short **o**
- recognizing and forming upper-case and lower-case **o**
- sound of **lŏ**
- words with short **o** in the middle
- formation of **ba**, **bo**, **do**, **dad**

Lesson 5

Letter **c**
- letter recognition
- sound of letter **c**
- words beginning with **c** and **că**
- recognizing and forming upper-case and lower-case **c**
- formation of **co**, **ca**

Lesson 6

Letter **e**
- letter recognition
- sound of short **e**
- words with **ĕ** in the middle
- matching phrases to pictures
- beginning sounds **dĕ** and **bĕ**
- word recognition and matching
- recognizing and forming upper-case and lower-case **e**
- matching letter to pictures starting with **ĕ**

Lesson 7

Letter **f**
- letter recognition
- sound of **f**
- beginning sounds **f**, **fă**, **fĕ**
- recognizing and forming upper-case and lower-case **f**
- reading and writing "make-up words"
- reading and writing short sentences

Lesson 8

Letter **g**
- letter recognition
- beginning sounds **g**, **gă**, **gŏ**
- words beginning and ending in **g**
- auditory discrimination from word list
- recognizing and forming upper-case and lower-case **g**
- matching letter to pictures starting with **g**
- reading and writing "make-up words"
- reading and writing short sentences

Lesson 9

Letter **i**
- letter recognition
- beginning sound of short **i**
- words with short **i** in the middle
- beginning consonant sounds
- middle vowel sounds
- recognizing and forming upper-case and lower-case **i**
- matching letter to pictures starting with **i**

Lesson 10

Letter h

- letter recognition
- beginning sounds **h**, **hă**, **hĕ**, **hŏ**, **hĭ**
- recognizing and forming upper-case and lower-case **h**
- reading and writing "make-up words"
- matching letter to pictures starting with **h**
- adding **s** to make plurals
- capital letter at beginning and period at end of sentence
- matching pictures to phrases

Lesson 11

Letter u

- letter recognition
- beginning sounds of **ŭ**, **dŭ**, **fŭ**, **bŭ**, **cŭ**, **gŭ**
- words with **ŭ** in the middle
- recognizing and forming upper-case and lower-case **u**
- matching letter to pictures with **ŭ** in the middle
- matching pictures to words

Lesson 12

Letter t

- letter recognition
- beginning and ending sound of **t**
- recognizing and forming upper-case and lower-case **t**
- matching letter to pictures starting with **t**
- reading and writing "make-up words"
- reading and printing sentences
- matching pictures to phrases
- recognition and printing **ta**, **te**, **ti**, **to**, **tu**

Lesson 13

Letter n

- letter recognition
- sound of **n**, **nă**
- matching pictures to words
- recognizing and forming upper-case and lower-case **n**

- matching letters to words starting with **n**
- spelling words to match pictures
- completing sentences with correct word
- printing words and phrases from copy
- identifying pictures starting with **ne**, **ni**, **nu**, **no**
- identifying pictures starting with **an**, **en**, **in**, **un**

Lesson 14

Letter k

- letter recognition
- beginning sounds **k**, **kĭ**, **kĕ**
- matching pictures to phrases
- recognizing and forming upper-case and lower-case **k**
- printing letters and words with **k**
- reading "make-up words"
- reading and printing sentences

Lesson 15

Letter l

- letter recognition
- beginning sounds **l**, **lă**, **lĕ**, **lĭ**, **lŏ**, **lŭ**
- ending sound of **l**
- recognizing and forming upper-case and lower-case **l**
- printing letters and words
- completing sentences with correct word
- reading "make-up words"

Lesson 16

Letter m

- recognizing and forming upper-case and lower-case **m**
- completing sentences with correct word
- spelling words to match pictures
- reading "make-up words"
- matching pictures to beginning sounds **ma**, **me**, **mi**, **mo**, **mu**
- reading and printing words and phrases from copy

Lesson 17

Letter **p**

- recognizing and forming upper-case and lower-case **p**
- beginning sounds of **pa**, **pe**, **pi**, **po**, **pu**
- matching pictures to words
- matching letters to words starting with **p**
- reading "make-up words"
- spelling words to match pictures
- printing words and phrases from copy
- completing sentences with correct word

Lesson 18

Letter **r**

- recognizing and forming upper-case and lower-case **r**
- matching letters to words starting with **r**
- reading "make-up words"
- beginning sounds of **ra**, **re**, **ri**, **ro**, **ru**
- matching pictures to words
- completing sentences with correct word
- spelling words to match pictures
- printing words and phrases from copy

Lesson 19

Letter **s**

- recognizing and forming upper-case and lower-case **s**
- matching letters to words starting with **s**
- beginning sounds of **sa**, **se**, **si**, **so**, **su**
- matching pictures to phrases
- recognizing ending sound of **s**
- printing letters, words, and phrases
- completing sentences with correct word

Lesson 20

Letter **q**

- recognizing and forming upper-case and lower-case **q**, **qu**, **qui**
- matching letters to words starting with **qu**
- match pictures to words
- reading and writing sentences

Lesson 21

Letter **j**

- recognizing and forming upper-case and lower-case **j**
- matching letters to words starting with **j**
- matching pictures to words
- completing sentences with correct word
- matching pictures to phrases
- beginning sounds of **ja**, **je**, **ji**, **jo**, **ju**
- spelling words to match pictures
- printing words and phrases from copy

Lesson 22

Letter **v**

- recognizing and forming upper-case and lower-case **v**
- matching letters to words starting with **v**
- spelling words to match pictures
- matching pictures to words and phrases
- beginning sounds of **va**, **ve**, **vi**, **vo**, **vu**
- completing sentences with correct word
- printing words and phrases from copy
- spelling words to match pictures

Lesson 23

Letter **w**

- recognizing and forming upper-case and lower-case **w**
- matching letters to words starting with **w**
- reading "make-up words"
- matching pictures to words and phrases
- printing words from copy
- completing sentences with correct word
- spelling words to match pictures
- reading and printing sentences

Lesson 24

Letter **y**

- recognizing and forming upper-case and lower-case **y**
- printing letters and words
- matching letters to words starting with **y**
- matching pictures to words and phrases

- completing sentences with correct word
- spelling words to match pictures

Lesson 25

Letter **z**

- recognizing and forming upper-case and lower-case **z**
- matching letters to words starting with **z**
- matching pictures to words
- reading "make-up words"
- recognizing words that end in **z**
- printing letters and words
- completing sentences with correct word
- printing phrases from copy

Lesson 26

Letter **x**

- recognizing and forming upper-case and lower-case **x**
- matching letters to words starting with **x**
- reading "make-up words"
- matching pictures to phrases, sentences, words
- words ending in **x**
- completing sentences with correct word
- spelling words to match pictures
- printing phrases from copy

Lesson 27

Consonant digraph **th**

- rule for beginning consonant digraph **th**
- matching picture to starting sound of **th**
- printing upper-case/lower-case **th**
- reading words/sentences
- identifying puzzle words and phrases
- rhyming and spelling
- reading and printing sentences from copy

Lesson 28

Consonant digraph **th**

- recognize **th** at the beginning or end of a word
- matching pictures to sentences

- printing sentences from copy
- reading "make-up" words
- puzzle words/phrases
- rhyming
- crossword puzzle with missing vowel

Lesson 29

Consonant digraph **ch**

- rule for consonant digraph **ch**
- matching pictures to sound
- using capital letters for names
- printing upper-case/lower-case **ch**
- reading sentences
- matching words/pictures
- matching puzzle words and phrases
- spelling

Lesson 30

Consonant digraph **wh**

- rule for consonant digraph **wh**
- identify capital and lower-case letters
- proper names
- identify nonsense words
- create nonsense words from sounds
- printing sentences from copy
- spelling
- use of question mark (?) and words to identify question sentences

Lesson 31

Review **th, ch, wh**

- picture/word review
- picture to sound
- printing
- auditory discrimination from word list
- spelling
- puzzle/"make-up" words and sentences
- recognizing words starting with ch within sentences

Lesson 32

Consonant digraph **sh**

- rule for beginning consonant digraph **sh**
- printing practice with capital and lower-case **sh**
- picture/word match
- puzzle/make-believe words and phrases
- word search
- printing sentences from copy
- rhyming
- spelling

Lesson 33

Consonant digraph **sh**

- rule for **sh** endings
- printing practice with and lower-case **sh**
- picture/beginning sound
- sentences to match picture
- rhyming
- alphabetize
- print sentences from copy
- identify sh at end of word

Lesson 34

Review consonant digraphs **th, ch, wh, sh**

- picture/sound identification
- printing/identifying ending sound
- word/picture identification
- auditory discrimination from word list
- spelling
- printing from copy

Lesson 35

Silent **e: ā ¢**

- rule for silent **e: a ¢**
- picture to sound
- diacritical marking
- short/long **a** contrast
- picture/sentence match
- puzzle/make-believe words and phrases
- spelling
- sentence completion
- word identification without pictures

Lesson 36

Consonant blend **bl**

- rule for blend **bl**
- picture to sound
- printing practice with capital and lower-case **bl**
- printing from copy
- picture to sentence match
- spelling
- word to picture match
- puzzle/make-believe words and phrases
- beginning blend choice

Lesson 37

Consonant blend **br**

- rule for blend **br**
- picture to sound
- printing practice with capital and lower-case **br**
- word identification – diacritical marking
- word/picture identification of sound
- sentence to picture match
- puzzle/make-believe words and sentences
- spelling
- sentence completion
- printing sentence from copy

Lesson 38

Consonant blend **cl**

- rule for blend **cl**
- picture to sound
- printing practice with capital and lower-case **cl**
- word/picture identification for printing
- beginning blend printing/spelling
- picture to word match
- puzzle/make-believe words and phrases
- printing sentence from copy

Lesson 39

Consonant blend **cr**
- rule for consonant blend **cr**
- picture to sound
- printing practice with capital and lower-case **cr**
- picture to word match
- printing beginning sounds
- word/picture identification for printing
- alphabetize
- sentence completion
- puzzle/make-believe words and phrases
- spelling

Lesson 40

Review consonant blends **cr**, **cl**, **br**, **bl**
- word/picture identification
- auditory discrimination from word list
- puzzle/make-believe words and phrases
- spelling – fill in beginning and ending sounds
- sentence printing from copy

Lesson 41

Silent **e**: ī ¢
- rule for silent **e**: ī ¢
- word/picture identification
- diacritical marking
- word/picture match
- sentence/picture match
- puzzle/make-believe words and phrases
- spelling

Lesson 42

Consonant blend **dr** – question sentences
- rule for consonant blend **dr**
- word/picture identification
- practice printing with capital and lower-case **dr**
- word/picture match
- printing beginning sounds for picture
- choice of beginning sounds
- puzzle/make-believe words and phrases

- rule for question marks and sentences
- review of question words and use of question marks
- spelling
- rhyming

Lesson 43

Consonant blend **fl**
- rule for consonant blend **fl**
- practice printing with capital and lower-case **fl**
- beginning sounds identified
- printing beginning sounds
- alphabetical order
- sentence completion
- puzzle/make-believe words and phrases
- sentence printing from copy

Lesson 44

Review silent **e**: ā ¢ and ī ¢ with single consonant beginnings
- review silent e rule
- diacritical marking
- picture/word identification
- printing – place in columns
- word/picture match
- auditory discrimination from word list
- spelling
- sentence completion

Lesson 45

Review silent **e**: ā ¢ and ī ¢ with consonant blend beginnings
- review silent **e** rule
- picture to sound – diacritical markings
- printing – place in columns
- word/picture match
- auditory discrimination from word list
- spelling
- sentence completion from pictures
- sentence completion – original

Lesson 46

Ending **ck**
- rule for **ck** ending
- picture/sound identification
- placement of sound within word
- picture/sentence match
- rhyming
- alphabetical order
- puzzle/make-believe words and phrases
- spelling

Lesson 47

Ending **ing**
- rule for **ing** ending
- picture to sound
- word identification
- picture to word match
- picture/sentence identification and printing
- word completion
- sentence completion
- printing
- auditory discrimination from word list

Lesson 48

Review short and long vowels
- short vowel identification
- long vowel identification
- word/picture match
- puzzle/make-believe words and phrases
- auditory discrimination for word list
- word comprehension from sentence
- spelling

Lesson 49

Silent **e**: ō ¢ – filling in sentences
- rule of silent **e**: ō ¢
- word/picture identification
- printing short and long vowel words - dia-critical marking
- word ending choice from pictures
- auditory discrimination from word list

- sentence completion
- rhyming
- puzzle and make believe words
- printing from copy

Lesson 50

Consonant blend **gr**
- rule for consonant blend **gr**
- word/picture match
- practice printing capital and lower case **gr**
- beginning sound identification
- word/picture match
- printing (spelling) beginning sounds from picture
- alphabetical order
- sentence completion
- puzzle/make-believe words and phrases
- word search

Lesson 51

Consonant blend **gl**
- rule for consonant blend **gl**
- word/picture match
- practice printing capital and lower case **gl**
- beginning sound identification
- alphabetical order
- ending sound identification
- auditory discrimination from word list
- sentence completion
- printing sentence from copy

Lesson 52

Consonant blend **sp** – beginning and ending
- rule for consonant blend **sp**
- word/picture match – beginning **sp**
- practice printing **sp** with capital
- word/picture match – ending **sp**
- sentence/picture match
- puzzle/make-believe words and phrases
- spelling and rhyming
- printing sentence from copy

Lesson 53

Consonant digraph ending **tch** and **ch**

- rule for consonant digraph **tch** and **ch**
- word/picture identification of sound
- word/picture match
- discrimination of **ch** and **tch**
- puzzle/make-believe words and phrases
- spelling
- auditory discrimination from word list
- crossword puzzle
- sentence printing from copy

Lesson 54

Review short vowels and silent **e**: $\bar{a}\ \cancel{e}$, $\bar{i}\ \cancel{e}$, $\bar{o}\ \cancel{e}$

- vowel identification
- diacritical marking
- change words from short to long vowel sounds
- words in columns – long **o**, **i**, **a**
- word/picture match
- word/sentence match
- rhyming

Lesson 55

Silent **e**: $\bar{u}\ \cancel{e}$

- review silent **e** rule
- word/picture identification
- print words to match pictures – copy
- sentence completion
- puzzle/make-believe words and phrases
- spelling
- separate columns for long vowel sounds
- auditory discrimination from word list

Lesson 56

Review short and long vowels with blends

- word/picture identification
- beginning or end sound identification
- sentence completion
- rhyming
- printing question sentence from copy

Lesson 57

Review short and long vowels with consonant single and blend beginning

- beginning sound identification/word/picture
- sentence completion
- printing sentence from copy

Lesson 58

Consonant endings **nd**, **nt** – nouns

- rule for consonant endings **nd**, **nt**
- word/picture identification
- printing
- consonant ending discrimination
- auditory discrimination from word list
- rule for nouns – person, thing
- noun identification
- noun recognition of name from sentences
- noun recognition of place from sentences
- word/picture comprehension choice

Lesson 59

Consonant ending **ng** – noun review

- word/picture identification
- printing
- ending sound identification from pictures
- auditory discrimination from word list
- noun identification
- sentence/picture comprehension choice
- rhyming
- printing sentence from copy

Lesson 60

Consonant ending **nk** – writing question sentences

- rule for consonant ending **nk**
- word/picture identification
- printing
- ending discrimination
- auditory discrimination from word list
- sentence completion
- rhyming

- yes/no to question sentences
- printing choice of question sentence

Lesson 61

Review consonant blends **ng**, **nk**, **nd**, **nt**
- word endings identification
- auditory discrimination from word list
- noun identification
- printing
- spelling
- alphabetical order

Lesson 62

Consonant blends **sc** and **sk** beginnings
- rule for consonant blends **sc** and **sk**
- word/picture identification – **sc**
- printing
- word/picture identification – **sk**
- auditory discrimination from word list
- picture/sentence comprehension
- nouns – sentence identification
- sentence comprehension, completion and identification from picture

Lesson 63

Consonant blend **sk** endings
- rule for consonant blend **sk** ending
- work/picture identification
- printing
- word/picture match
- auditory discrimination from word list
- rhyming
- word/picture identification
- spelling
- sentence/picture comprehension
- alphabetical order

Lesson 64

Consonant blend **mp** endings – sentences
- rule for consonant blend **mp** endings
- picture/word identification
- printing
- word/picture discrimination

- auditory discrimination
- rhyming
- rule for description of sentence structure
- exclamation sentences
- question sentences
- statement sentences
- printing choice of sentences from copy

Lesson 65

Consonant ending **lp** – question sentences
- picture/word association
- printing
- picture/word discrimination
- printing choice from pictures – punctuation – question mark – period
- introduction to action words
- writing from copy with choice of action words
- spelling
- auditory discrimination from word list

Lesson 66

Consonant ending **lk** – vocabulary
- rule for consonant ending **lk**
- picture/word discrimination
- spelling choice for sentence completion and comprehension
- auditory discrimination from word list
- word/picture match
- spelling – ending sounds
- picture/sentence comprehension
- printing sentences from copy – punctuation

Lesson 67

Review endings **sk**, **mp**, **lp**, **lk** with short vowels
- picture/ending sound identification
- printing
- spelling
- auditory discrimination from word list
- sentence completion
- alphabetical order

Lesson 68

Review consonant blends
- word/picture identification
- beginning or ending sound discrimination
- spelling
- alphabetical order
- sentence completion
- rhyming
- writing sentence from copy

Lesson 69

Beginning consonant blend **pl** – pronouns
- rule for consonant blend **pl**
- word/picture identification
- practice printing **pl** with capital and lower-case letters
- picture/word beginning sound identification
- picture/word match
- alphabetical order
- Review noun rule
- rule – pronoun
- read sentences – change from noun to pronoun
- write sentence from copy – identify pronoun

Lesson 70

Review beginning consonant blends
- picture/beginning sound identification
- printing
- noun identification
- pronoun identification
- creative sentence making

Lesson 71

Double vowels – **ai**
- rule for double vowels – **ai**
- picture/sound identification
- word/picture match
- print rhyming words from copy
- puzzle/make-believe words and phrases
- sentence completion
- spelling
- printing sentence from copy

Lesson 72

Consonant blends with **ai**
- picture/sound identification
- printing
- puzzle/make-believe words and phrases
- picture/word and sound discrimination
- sentence/picture match
- sentence completion
- alphabetical order

Lesson 73

Consonant blend beginnings **pr, tr** – quotation marks
- rule for consonant blend beginnings **pr** and **tr**
- picture/word sound discrimination
- printing
- pictures/choice of beginning sounds
- word/picture match
- rule for quotation marks.
- read sentences
- print sentences using quotation marks

Lesson 74

Consonant blend beginning **sl**
- rule for consonant blend **sl**
- picture/word sound discrimination
- practice printing letters – capital and lower-case
- picture/beginning sound association
- picture/word match
- spelling
- puzzle/make-believe words and phrases
- create puzzle words

Lesson 75

Consonant blend beginning **sm**
- rule for consonant blend **sm**
- picture/word sound discrimination

- practice printing letters – capital and lower-case
- word/picture match
- sentence/picture match
- rhyming
- quotation marks
- spelling
- alphabetical order

Lesson 76

Consonant blend **sn**
- rule for consonant blend **sn**
- picture/word sound discrimination
- practice printing letters – capital and lower-case
- word/picture match
- sentence/picture match
- rhyming
- picture/sentence comprehension
- auditory discrimination from word list

Lesson 77

Review of consonant blends and digraphs
- pictures/sound discrimination
- auditory discrimination from word list
- auditory discrimination identifying ending sounds

Lesson 78

Double vowels – **ea**
- rule for double vowels **ea**
- picture/sound identification
- picture – printing and diacritical marking
- picture/word match
- puzzle/make-believe words and phrases
- rhyming
- sentence completion
- spelling
- printing sentence from copy

Lesson 79

Double vowels – **ee**
- rule for double vowels **ee**
- picture/sound identification

- picture – printing and diacritical marking
- picture/word match
- rhyming
- puzzle/make-believe words and phrases
- sentence/picture match
- spelling
- printing sentence from copy

Lesson 80

Beginning **qu** – picture sequence
- rule for **qu**
- picture/sound identification
- practice printing with capital and lower-case
- picture/word match
- rhyming
- sentence/picture match
- picture sequence

Lesson 81

Beginning blend **scr** – picture sequence
- picture/sound identification
- practice printing with capital and lower-case
- picture/word match
- printing sentence from copy – quotation marks
- spelling
- sentence sequence
- yes/no questions

Lesson 82

Review of double vowels – beginning blends
- picture/sound identification
- auditory discrimination from word list
- spelling
- picture/sentence comprehension
- sentence completion

Lesson 83

Double vowels – **oa**
- review double vowel rule – include **oa**
- picture/sound identification
- printing – diacritical marking

- word/picture match
- rhyming
- puzzle/make-believe words and phrases
- sentence comprehension/pictures
- spelling
- printing sentence from copy

Lesson 84

Beginning blend **fr**

- rule for beginning blend **fr**
- picture/sound identification
- practice printing with capital and lower-case
- picture/word match
- rhyming
- puzzle/make-believe words and phrases
- printing for sentence completion
- spelling
- yes/no sentence
- printing sentence from copy

Lesson 85

Consonant endings **lt, lf**

- rule for consonant ending **lt** and **lf**
- picture/sound identification
- reading – sentence comprehension
- auditory discrimination
- spelling
- printing – punctuation
- picture/sentence match

Lesson 86

Consonant ending **ft** – following directions

- rule for consonant ending **ft**
- picture/sound identification
- printing
- word ending sound identification
- auditory discrimination from word list
- picture/sentence comprehension
- follow directions
- word/picture match

Lesson 87

Review consonant endings

- pictures/sound identification
- sentence completion
- rhyme/picture
- auditory discrimination from word list
- spelling

Lesson 88

Review long and short vowel sounds

- picture/sound identification
- change word from short to long – diacritical marking
- column choice for words
- sentence completion

Lesson 89

Consonant blend beginnings **spr, spl**

- rule for consonant blend beginnings **spr, spl**
- picture/sound identification
- practice printing with capital and lower-case
- picture/sound discrimination
- word to word match
- read sentences from copy – print quotation marks
- alphabetical order
- sentence sequence for story

Lesson 90

Consonant blend beginning **st**

- rule for consonant blend beginning **st**
- picture/sound identification
- practice printing with capital and lower-case
- picture/word match
- rhyming
- puzzle/make-believe words and phrases
- sentence completion
- yes/no choice
- spelling

Lesson 91

Consonant blend review – **tch, sp, ft**
- ending sound identification
- printing
- picture/sentence comprehension match
- read sentences – vocabulary comprehension
- rhyming
- yes/no choice
- printing sentence from copy

Lesson 92

Consonant blend ending **st**
- rule for consonant blend ending **st**
- printing
- picture/sound identification
- auditory discrimination from word list
- rhyming
- reading sentences – vocabulary enrichment
- spelling
- sentence completion

Lesson 93

Review consonant endings – **tch, sp, st, lt, lf, ft**
- picture/sound identification
- auditory discrimination from word list
- sentence completion
- rhyming
- spelling – end sounds
- sentence choice to match picture

Lesson 94

Consonant blends **tw, sw**
- picture/sound identification
- puzzle/make-believe words and sentences
- printing sentence from copy
- sentence completion
- yes/no choice
- spelling

Lesson 95

Review consonant beginnings **tw, sp, st, spl, spr, qu**
- picture/sound identification
- auditory discrimination from word list
- sentence completion
- rhyming
- spelling
- yes/no choice
- alphabetical order
- print sentences – quotation marks

Lesson 96

Review endings **lf, ft, ng, nk, lk, lp, sk, sh**
- picture/sound discrimination
- sentence completion
- alphabetical order
- spelling
- could be/no way
- columns for endings
- read sentences – vocabulary development

Lesson 97

Vowel plus **r: ar**
- rule for vowel plus **r: ar**
- picture/sound identification
- practice printing with lower-case
- sentence/picture match – **ar** recognition
- rhyming
- puzzle/make-believe words and phrases
- read sentences – vocabulary development
- word search

Lesson 98

Vowel plus **r: or**
- rule for vowel plus **r: or**
- picture/sound identification
- practice printing with lower-case
- sentence/picture match – **or** recognition
- puzzle/make-believe words and phrases
- read sentences – vocabulary development
- sentence completion
- printing sentences – capitals/punctuation

Lesson 99

Review vowel plus **r**: **ar**, **or**

- picture/sound identification
- practice printing
- sentence completion
- alphabetical order
- spelling
- could be/no way
- read sentences – vocabulary development
- auditory discrimination from word list

Lesson 100

Review vowel plus **r**: **ar**

- picture/sound identification
- spelling
- sentence completion
- sentence/picture match – identify **ar**
- puzzle/make-believe words and phrases
- auditory discrimination from word list
- read sentences – vocabulary development

Lesson 101

Review vowel plus **r**: **or**

- picture/sound identification
- spelling
- sentence completion
- alphabetical order
- yes/no choice
- read sentences – vocabulary development
- crossword puzzle

Lesson 102

Vowel plus **r**: **er**, **ir**, **ur**

- rule for vowel plus **r**: **er**, **ir**, **ur**
- sound identification from written word
- printing
- picture/sentence match – **er** sound identification
- puzzle/make-believe words and phrases
- read sentences – vocabulary development
- could be/no way

Lesson 103

Vowel plus **r**: **ir**

- review rule for vowel plus **r**: **ir**
- sound identification from written word
- printing
- picture/sentence match – **ir** sound identification
- puzzle/make-believe words and phrases
- read sentences – vocabulary development
- auditory discrimination

Lesson 104

Vowel plus **r**: **ur**

- review rule for vowel plus **r**: **ur**
- printing
- picture/sentence match – **ur** sound identification
- puzzle/make-believe words and phrases
- read sentences – vocabulary development
- sound identification

Lesson 105

Review vowel plus **r**: **er**, **ir**, **ur**

- picture/sound association
- sentence completion
- printing
- sentence/picture match – sound identification
- words in column
- rhyming
- auditory discrimination from word list
- could be/no way

Lesson 106

Review vowel plus **r**: **ar**, **or**

- picture/sound association
- sentence completion
- alphabetical order
- picture/sentence match
- words in columns
- yes/no
- rhyming

Lesson 107

Review all vowels plus **r**
- picture/sound association
- sentence completion
- alphabetical order
- rhyming
- picture/sentence match
- word/picture match

Lesson 108

Plurals – **s**
- rule for plurals – **s**
- singular and plural identification
- spelling
- picture/phrase match
- sentence completion
- pictures – choice of plurals or singular

Lesson 109

Plurals – **es**
- rule for plurals – **es**
- spelling
- picture/phrase match
- sentence completion
- pictures – choice of plurals or singular

Lesson 110

Plurals – **y** into **ies**
- rule for **y** into **ies**
- spelling
- picture – plural identification
- phrase/picture match
- sentence completion
- pictures – choice of plurals or singular

Lesson 111

Review plurals – **s**, **es**, **ies**
- plural identification
- spelling
- word identification with plurals
- sentence/picture match – identify plurals

Lesson 112

Review double vowels – **ee**
- review rule for double vowels – **ee**
- picture/sound identification
- print/diacritical markings
- word/picture match
- rhyming
- puzzle/make-believe words and phrases
- sentence comprehension
- spelling
- alphabetical order

Lesson 113

Review double vowels – **ee**, **oa** – apostrophe
- picture/sound association
- printing – diacritical markings
- sentence completion
- spelling
- rhyming
- rule for apostrophe – possession
- sentence exchange – single possession
- sentence exchange – plural possession

Lesson 114

Review double vowels – **ai**, **ea**
- picture/sound association
- column printing
- sentence completion
- spelling
- review apostrophe rule
- sentence exchange – single possession
- sentence exchange – plural possession

Lesson 115

Review all double vowels
- picture/sound association
- printing – diacritical markings
- sentence completion
- puzzle/make-believe words and phrases
- spelling

Lesson 116

Digraph **ay**

- rule for digraph **ay**
- picture/sound association
- printing
- rhyming
- puzzle/make-believe words and phrases
- sentence comprehension
- spelling
- alphabetical order

Lesson 117

Digraph **ey**

- rule for digraph **ey**
- picture/sound association
- printing – diacritical marking
- read sentences – vocabulary development
- rhyming
- puzzle/make-believe words and phrases
- alphabetical order

Lesson 118

Review digraphs **ay**, **ey** – apostrophe

- review digraph rule – **ay**, **ey**
- word/sound association
- sentence completion
- picture/word match
- spelling
- review apostrophe rule
- print sentence exchange for single possession
- print sentence exchange for plural possession

Lesson 119

Diphthong **ow**

- rule for diphthong **ow**
- word/sound association
- picture/word match
- sentence completion
- auditory determination from word list
- printing from copy

Lesson 120

Diphthong **ou**

- rule for both sounds of **ou**
- picture/sound association
- sentence completion
- printing sentences from copy – identify punctuation

Lesson 121

Review digraphs **ay**, **ey**

- picture/sound association
- word/picture match
- spelling
- sentence completion
- noun identification
- sentence sequence
- alphabetical order
- picture/sentence match – **ay**, **ey** identified
- auditory discrimination from word list
- make-believe sentences

Lesson 122

Review digraphs **ay**, **ey**; diphthongs **ow**, **ou**

- picture/word association
- spelling
- sentence completion
- word/picture match – sound identification
- auditory discrimination from word bank
- make-believe phrase

Lesson 123

Digraphs **aw**, **au** – proper nouns – creative writing

- rule for digraphs **aw**, **au**
- picture/sound association
- picture/word match
- word/sound association
- spelling
- sentence completion
- printing – punctuation
- creative writing

- sentence printing – proper nouns
- make-believe phrase

Lesson 124

Digraph **ew**

- rule for digraph **ew**
- picture/sound association
- picture/word match
- spelling
- sentence completion
- review proper nouns
- rule for common noun
- common nouns in sentences
- printing sentences – quotation marks
- auditory discrimination
- make-believe phrase

Lesson 125

Diphthong **oy**

- rule for diphthong **oy**
- picture/sound association
- spelling
- word/picture match
- sentence completion
- proper and common noun identification
- quotation marks
- alphabetical order
- printing
- auditory discrimination from word list

Lesson 126

Review digraphs **aw**, **au**, **ew**; diphthong **oy**

- picture/sound association
- picture/word match
- auditory discrimination from word list
- sentence completion
- printing
- rhyming

Lesson 127

Diphthong **oi**

- rule for diphthong **oi**
- picture/sound association
- picture/word match

- printing
- sentences – sound identification
- make-believe phrases
- spelling
- sentences – vocabulary development
- printing – punctuation

Lesson 128

Review diphthongs **ow**, **ou**; digraphs **ay**, **ey**

- picture/sound association
- sentence completion
- alphabetical order
- rhyming
- sentence/picture match
- printing – punctuation
- auditory discrimination from word list

Lesson 129

Review digraphs **aw**, **au**, **ew**

- picture/sound association
- sentence completion
- picture/word match
- sentences – quotation marks
- auditory discrimination from word list
- spelling
- make-believe phrases

Lesson 130

Review **ow**, **ou**

- picture/sound association
- picture/word match
- spelling
- sentences – sound discrimination
- make-believe phrase
- sentences – punctuation
- auditory discrimination from word list

Lesson 131

Review diphthongs **oy**, **oi**

- picture/sound association
- picture/word match
- spelling
- auditory discrimination from word list
- sentences – sound discrimination

- sentence/picture match
- rhyming
- printing/punctuation

Lesson 132

Letter **y** as in **cry**
- rule for letter **y** as in **cry**
- picture/sound association
- spelling
- word/picture match
- read sentences – vocabulary development
- rhyming
- sentence completion
- auditory discrimination from word list
- printing

Lesson 133

Letter **y** as in **baby**
- rule for Letter **y** as in **baby**
- picture/sound association
- spelling
- word/picture match
- read sentences – vocabulary development
- rhyming
- sentence completion
- auditory discrimination from word list
- printing sentence

Lesson 134

Review Letter **y** as in **cry**, **baby**
- review letter **y** sounds
- picture/sound association
- column printing
- sentence completion
- capitalization – proper nouns
- spelling
- auditory discrimination from word list

Lesson 135

Vowel digraph – special **oo** as in **book**
- rule for vowel digraph – **oo** as in **book**
- picture/printing

- read sentences/sound association
- printing
- auditory discrimination from word list
- rhyming
- read sentences – vocabulary development

Lesson 136

Vowel digraph – special **oo** as in **tooth**
- Rule for vowel digraph – special **oo** as in **tooth**
- picture/printing
- read sentences/sound association
- printing
- auditory discrimination from word list
- rhyming
- read sentences – vocabulary development
- printing sentence from copy

Lesson 137

Review all digraphs/diphthongs
- spelling
- sentence/picture match
- common nouns

Lesson 138

Review letter **y** – long **i** and **e**
- spelling
- sentence completion
- rhyming
- auditory discrimination from word list

Lesson 139

Silent letter **w**
- rule for silent **w**
- picture/word association
- spelling
- printing
- sentences/word identification
- auditory discrimination from word list
- picture description
- make-believe phrase

Lesson 140

Silent letter **k**

- rule for silent **k**
- picture/word association
- spelling
- printing
- make-believe phrase
- auditory discrimination
- sentences – word identification
- picture description

Lesson 141

Silent letter **b**

- rule for silent **b**
- picture/word association
- spelling
- printing
- make-believe phrase
- auditory discrimination from word list
- sentences – word identification
- word discrimination

Lesson 142

Review silent letters **b**, **k**, **w**

- word identification
- word/picture match
- spelling
- auditory discrimination from word list
- sentence/picture match
- identify silent letters
- letter writing

Lesson 143

Silent letter **g**

- rule for silent **g**
- printing
- spelling
- word discrimination
- sentence/picture match
- auditory discrimination from word list
- spelling
- picture description
- questions

Lesson 144

Silent **gh**

- rule for silent **gh**
- word/picture association
- spelling
- phrase match
- auditory discrimination from word list
- sentence/picture match
- puzzle picture

Lesson 145

Review silent letters – **w**, **k**, **b**, **gn**, **gh**

- word/picture identification
- column printing
- auditory discrimination from word list
- word identification
- story comprehension
- creative sentence writing

Lesson 146

le endings

- rule for words ending in le
- word/picture identification
- printing
- word/picture match
- sentence/word identification
- make-believe phrase
- sentence completion
- story comprehension

Lesson 147

Words with **all**

- rule for words with **all**
- word/picture association
- printing
- word/picture match
- spelling
- sentence/word identification
- make-believe phrases
- sentence/comprehension
- story comprehension
- creative sentence writing

Lesson 148

Syllables – double consonants

- rule for double consonants
- word/picture identification
- printing
- sentence/word discrimination

Lesson 149

Syllables – compound words

- rule for syllables with compound words
- word/picture identification
- printing compound words
- word-parts match
- sentences word identification
- make-believe phrase
- word identification
- compound word identification

Lesson 150

Syllables – consonant between vowels

- rule for syllables
- syllable recognition
- printing
- sentences/syllable recognition
- auditory discrimination from word list
- make-believe phrases
- sentences – punctuation
- picture sequence

Lesson 151

Review syllables

- compound word identification
- word/picture match
- sentence completion
- creative sentences using compound words
- creative sentences using double consonants

Lesson 152

Suffix **ing** – prepositions

- signal for word ending with ing
- word/picture match
- spelling
- sentence completion – base word
- rule for prepositions
- picture/identify prepositional phrases

Lesson 153

Special soft **c**

- rule for soft **c**
- reading/printing
- word/picture match
- spelling
- sentences/word identification
- sentence completion
- review noun rule
- identify nouns in sentences
- creative writing of nouns

Lesson 154

Special soft **g**

- rule for soft **g**
- reading/printing
- word/picture match
- spelling
- column printing
- alphabetical order
- make-believe phrases
- sentences/word identification
- picture sequence

Lesson 155

Review ending **ing**, soft **c**, soft **g**

- base word completion
- sentence completion
- picture/word choice
- sentence completion
- sentence sequence
- creative sentence

Lesson 156

Non-phonetic **alk**, **ph** – contractions

- rule for **ph**
- picture/word identification
- printing
- word/picture match

- spelling
- sentence completion
- rule for words with **alk**
- picture/word
- read sentences/vocabulary development
- rule for contractions
- words for contractions
- creative use of contractions

Lesson 157

Non-phonetic **old**, **ost**, **olt**

- rule for non-phonetic word parts – **old**, **ost**, **olt**
- picture/word identification
- printing
- word/picture match
- read sentences/vocabulary development
- action verbs
- sentence completion
- sentence/picture match – action verb identified
- creative action verb

Lesson 158

Non-phonetic **ild**, **ind**

- rule for non-phonetic word parts – **ild**, **ind**
- picture/word identification
- printing
- spelling
- sentence completion
- nouns: proper, common
- pronouns
- verbs
- creative sentences

Lesson 159

Review non-phonetic word parts – **alk**, **old**, **ost**, **olt**, **ind**, **ild**

- picture/word match
- printing
- spelling
- picture/word completion choice
- sentence completion
- crossword puzzle
- auditory discrimination

Lesson 160

Review all

- spelling
- plurals
- double vowels
- silent **e**
- picture/word match
- diacritical markings
- double consonants
- syllables
- compound words
- soft **c** and **g**
- picture/word match

Teacher's Lessons

Lesson 41 - Silent e: ī ȩ́

Overview:

- Review all long vowel sounds
- Review Phonics Rules
- Review Silent **e** Rule
- Introduce silent **e** with long **i** sound
- Introduce familiar word families
- Compare short and long vowels

Materials and Supplies:

- Teacher's Guide & Student Workbook
- White board
- Reader 2: *Dick's Bike Ride*

Teaching Tips:

Introduce familiar word families with **i** and the silent **e**: **ide, ike, ile, ime, ine, ipe, ire**.

Explain the difference between short **i** and long **i** sound in word change: **dim – dime**.

Activity 1. List vowels **a, i, o,** and **u** on the white board with diacritical markings. Review the Silent **e** Rule: When two vowels are close together in a word, the FIRST one says its own name and the other one is silent as in **bake, dine, rode, tune**. Use diacritical markings with a crossed out **e**, and a straight line (macron) above the first vowel.

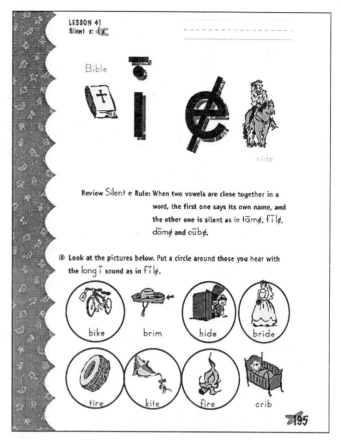

Study the pictures together and discuss the meanings for vocabulary development. Discuss family endings: **-ide, -ike, -ile, -ime, -ine, -ipe, -ire**. Have the student put a circle around those that have the long **i** sound.

Pictures: **bike, brim, hide, bride
tire, kite, fire, crib**

Activity 2. On the white board, have the students print the words with short **i**, then add the silent **e**: **pin** to **pine**, **Tim** to **time**. As soon as they understand the concept, have the student print the words with short **i**, and then add the silent **e**. They will use the diacritical marking to cross out the **e** and make a straight line over the long vowel **i**.

Pictures: **pin to pine, kit to kite, Tim to time
rip to ripe, fin to fine, fir to fire**

Activity 3. Study the pictures together and discuss the ending sound of each. Have the student print the word below the picture. Student will then cross out the silent **e** and put a straight line over the vowel **i** to show it has the long **i** sound.

Words: **ride, pipe, dime, pie**

Activity 4. Study the words and the pictures together and discuss the meanings. Have the student draw a line from the word to the picture it matches.

Pictures: **pine, kite, shine, dime, fire**

Activity 5. Read the sentences together and discuss the pictures. Have the student draw a line to match the picture.

Pictures: **Mike has time to fix his tire.
Jane can hide in a shed.
Jake has a dime in his hand.
Ike has a red and white kite.**

Activity 6. Read the make-up words.

Make-up Words: **brife, blape, chade, thide**

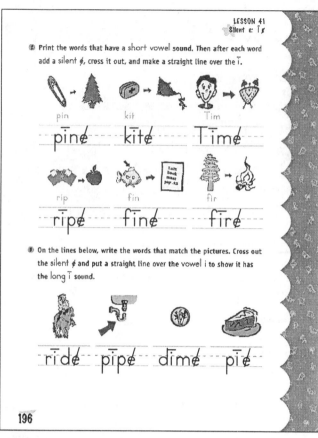

Activity 7. Read the puzzle phrases together. Have the student draw a line from the puzzle phrase to the picture it matches.

Pictures: **wipe a dime**
bite a pine
a pipe on a hike
a bride on a vine

Activity 8. Demonstrate on the white board how to complete a word by adding the missing vowel. Have the student finish spelling the words by inserting the long vowel sound under the pictures.

Words/pictures: five, ride, bike, pie
time, line, pipe, nine

Lesson 42 - Consonant Blend dr

Overview:

- Review all long vowel sounds
- Review Phonetic Rules
- Review Silent **e** Rule
- Introduce consonant blend **dr**
- Review use of question sentences
- Use of question marks.

Materials and Supplies:

- Teacher's Guide & Student Workbook
- White board
- Reader 2: *Drake's Drawings*

Teaching Tips:

Demonstrate the correct sound of **dr**. A picture of a **dress** can be used as an example of the sound. Use the white board to demonstrate the use of the blend **dr** with the vowels following.

For question sentences and the use of question marks, verbalize questions in which the student must make an answer. Introduce making a question mark when printing. Show the difference between a telling sentence and a question sentence.

Activity 1. Review the Short Vowel Rule and the Silent **e** Rule. Use the board to demonstrate the use of short vowels following **dr**: **dra**, **dre**, **dri**, **dro**. Indicate that the Silent **e** Rule is used as in **drake** and **drive**. Study the pictures together to identify the beginning sound. Have the student put a circle around the picture that starts with the sound of **dr**.

Pictures: **drum, dress, drive, crane
class, draw, drip, drill**

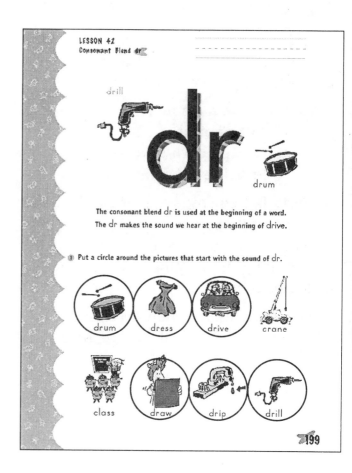

Activity 2. Use the white board to practice printing the blend with both capital **D** and lower-case **d**. Have the students practice printing **Dr** with a capital **D**.

Activity 3. Practice printing **dr** with lower-case letters.

Activity 4. Study and read the words together. Have the student draw a line from the word to the picture it matches.

    Pictures: **drum, dress, thin, drip**

Activity 5. Study the pictures and their meaning. Have the student print the beginning consonant blends for each word below the picture.

    Pictures: **br**ick, **sh**ip, **cr**ib

Activity 6. Review consonants blends again. Study the pictures to be able to identify the beginning sound. From the choice of four blends, have the student circle the one that begins the word for each picture.

    Pictures: **dr**um, **cr**ust, **br**ide, **cl**ip
            clock, **dr**ill, **cl**ub, **cr**ack

Activity 7. Read the make-up words.

    Make-up Words: **dris, drem, drof, drub, drap**

Activity 8. Read the puzzle phrases together. Have the student draw a line from each puzzle phrase to the picture it matches.

    Pictures: **a drum in a crib**
           a drill with a drip
           a dog can drive
           a dress with a crack

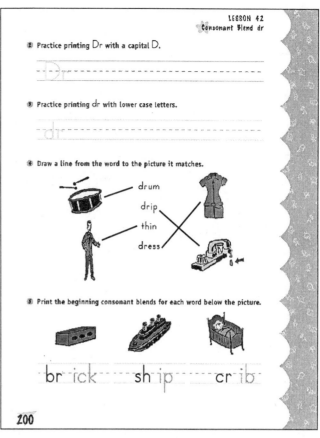

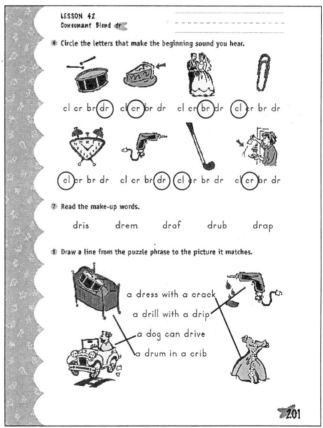

Activity 9. Students have been exposed to the idea of question sentences. This activity will help the student determine the use of the words that create a question sentence. The student should have an opportunity to practice writing a question mark on the white board. Have the student ask a question, the teacher writes it on the white board, and the student puts the question mark at the end of the sentence.

In Activity 9, read the question sentences together and have the student print the question mark at the end of the sentence. Have the student create the answer to the question.

1. Who came to the lake [**?**]
2. Where is the dress [**?**]
3. What time is it [**?**]
4. When did Mom get here [**?**]

Activity 10. Have the student determine if the sentence is a question or a telling sentence. Student will print the correct punctuation for each sentence.

1. What did you do [**?**]
2. Where did Jane go [**?**]
3. I have a ball [**.**]
4. I went to get a drink [**.**]
5. When will Brad go home [**?**]
6. Who will brush the dog [**?**]

Activity 11. Study the pictures and discuss the beginning sounds for each picture. Have the student print the beginning sound for the word under each picture.

Pictures: **dr**ill, **dr**ive, **dr**ip
         brush, **bl**ack, **cl**ip

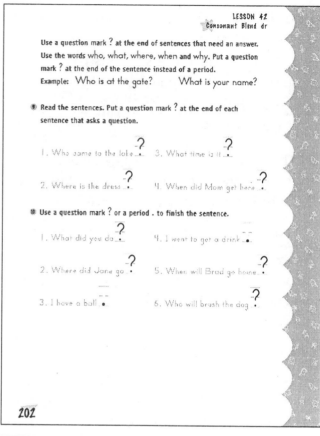

Activity 12. Review the rules for rhyming. On the white board print endings of words and have the student supply single letters or beginning blends to make a real or a make-up word. Let the student print the words on the white board.

Read the words together in the word bank. Have the student choose and print the rhyming words in the column that rhymes.

rug/**mug, drug**
raft/**craft, draft**
chill/**drill, mill**
brag/**drag, rag**
rip/**drip, chip**

Lesson 43 - Consonant Blend fl

Overview:

- Review all long vowel sounds
- Review Phonetic Rules
- Review Silent **e** Rule
- Introduce consonant blend **fl**
- Alphabetize

Materials and Supplies:

- Teacher's Guide & Student Workbook
- White board
- Reader 2: *A Tube for Floating*

Teaching Tips:

Demonstrate the correct sound of **fl**. A picture of the **flag** can be used as an example of the sound. Use the white board to demonstrate the use of the blend **fl** with the vowels following.

Activity 1. Review the Short Vowel Rule and the Silent **e** Rule. Use the board to demonstrate the use of short vowels following **fl**: **fla, fle, fli, flo, flu**. Indicate that the Silent **e** Rule is used as in **flake** and **flame**. Study the pictures together to identify the beginning sound. Have the student put a circle around each picture that starts with the sound **fl**.

Pictures: **flag, flash, drum, floor**
float, fly, flame, dress

Activity 2. Use the white board to practice printing the blend with both capital **F** and lower-case **f**. Have the student practice printing **Fl** with a capital **F**.

Activity 3. Have the student practice printing **fl** with a lower case **f**.

Activity 4. Review the consonant blends again. Study the pictures to be able to identify the beginning sound. From the choice of five blends, have the student circle the one that begins the word for each picture.

Pictures: **fl**ame, **cl**own, **dr**ive
brush, **dr**ess, **br**ick

Activity 5. Study the pictures together. Discuss the beginning blends. Have the student spell the beginning blend sounds to complete the words below the pictures.

Pictures: **fl**ag, **cl**ass, **dr**ess, **bl**ack

Activity 6. Study the pictures together to determine the beginning consonant blend. Have the student spell the word on the lines below the pictures if the word begins with the **fl** sound.

Pictures: **flash, flame, flip
flat, flock, flag**

Activity 7. Review alphabetical order. Have the students read the words. Print the letters **b, c, d, f**, on the white board. Have the student print the words under the appropriate letter on the white board. When the concept is understood, have the student print the words in alphabetical order in the workbook.

Words: **baby, cat, dog, flag**

Activity 8. Read the sentences and the words in the word bank together. Discuss the appropriate blank to print the word. Try each word from the word bank in the sentences. Have the student print the word in the blanks to make the sentence correct.

l.Tom can (**flip**) his legs.
2.The (**drake**) is on the lake.
3.Mike has a red, white, and blue (**flag**).
4.Jake had a (**fire**) in the sand.

Activity 9. Read the make-up words.

Make-up Words: **flig, flime, flane, flup,
fleb**

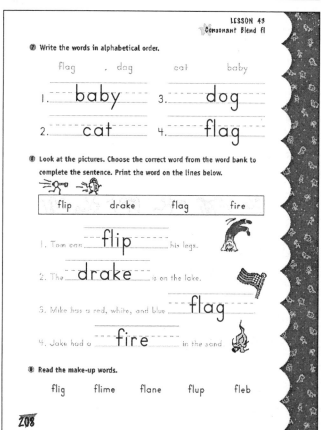

Lesson 44 - Review
Silent e: ā e̸ & ī e̸

Overview:

- Review all long vowel sounds
- Review Phonetic Rules
- Review Silent **e** Rule with ā e̸ and ī e̸.

Materials and Supplies:

- Teacher's Guide & Student Workbook
- White board
- Reader 2: *Jake's Bike*

Teaching Tips:

Use the white board to review the Silent **e** Rule with ā e̸ and ī e̸. Review the Silent **e** Rule. Use the board again to evaluate the student's ability to distinguish between short and long vowels as used in a word.

Activity 1. Review the Silent **e** Rule with long **a**. Discuss the pictures and have the student put a circle around those you hear with the long **a** sound.

Pictures: **wave, cake, rake, ant**
 cut, game, cane, cave

Activity 2. Study the pictures together. Discuss the pictures and their meaning. Have the student put a circle around those that have the long **i** sound.

Pictures: **fire, pipe, bike, bite**
 mile, time, tire, dig

Activity 3. Review the Silent **e** Rule with ā e̸ and ī e̸. Read the words in the word bank together. Have the student determine in which column the words will be printed.

Long **a** Words: **lake, bake, wave**
Long **i** Words: **Mike, file, time**

Activity 4. Study the pictures and read the words together. Have the student draw a line from the word to the picture it matches.

Pictures: **cane, game, dime, vase, hive**

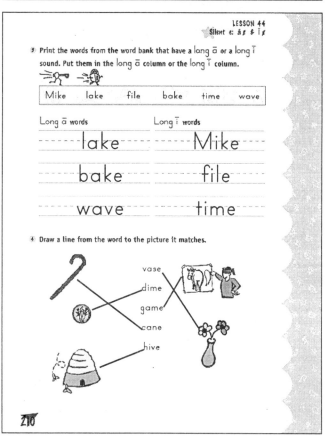

Activity 5. Read one word from each of the boxes. Student is to circle the correct word then print the circled words on the line below.

Words: **bake, bike, mile**
vase, dike, dame
same, tame, ride
line, tape, dive

Activity 6. Use the white board to practice spelling. Teacher will write the beginning and ending sounds, leaving the vowel sound in the middle blank for the student to complete. Practice with several long **i** and long **e** words. When the concept is understood, have the student spell the words below the pictures by printing the correct long vowel sound.

Pictures/words: r**a**ke, t**i**me, b**i**ke
t**a**pe, p**i**pe, g**a**me

Activity 7. Read the words in the word bank together and discuss the meaning of each. Read the sentences together and try the various words for each blank.

1. Jake will (**wave**) to Bill.
2. Mike has a (**bike**) to ride.
3. The (**game**) is fun for Sam.
4. Take a bite of (**pie**).

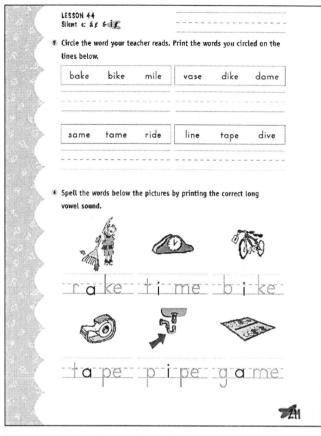

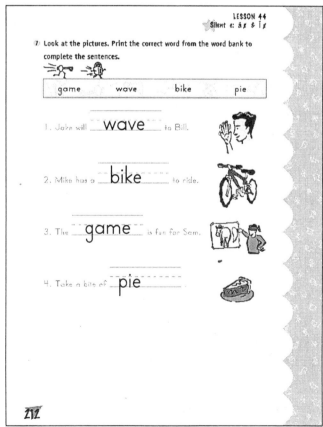

Lesson 45 - Review Silent e: ā ȇ & ī ȇ with Blends

Overview:

- Review all long vowel sounds
- Review Phonetic Rules
- Review consonant blends
- Review Silent **e** Rule with **ā ȇ** and **ī ȇ**.

Material and Supplies:

- Teacher's Guide & Student Workbook
- White board
- Reader 2: *Shine*

Teaching Tips:

Use the white board to review the Silent **e** Rule. Review consonant blends with all short vowels. Concentrate study and review on long vowels with blends and single beginning consonants. Use the board again to evaluate the student's ability to distinguish between short and long vowels as used in a word.

Activity 1. Review the pictures together. Have the student put a circle around those that have a long **a** sound.

Pictures: **drake, shave, blade, hide milk, brake, wave, flame**

Activity 2. Review the pictures together. Have the student put a circle around those you hear with a long **i** sound.

Pictures: **drive, dime, flash, bride shine, fin, nine, hike**

Activity 3. Use the white board to review blends used with long **a** and **e**. Teacher will write the beginning sounds on the board and the student can print the remaining part of the word. When the concept is maintained, have the student read the words in the word bank and print under the columns as indicated.

Long ā Words: **brake, drake, crate**
Long ī Words: **drive, bride, white**

38

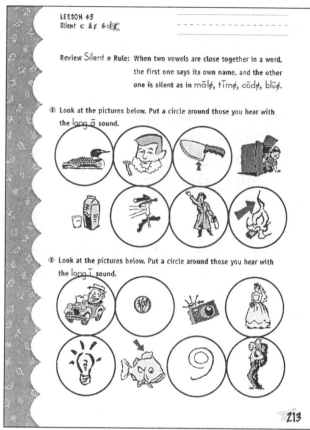

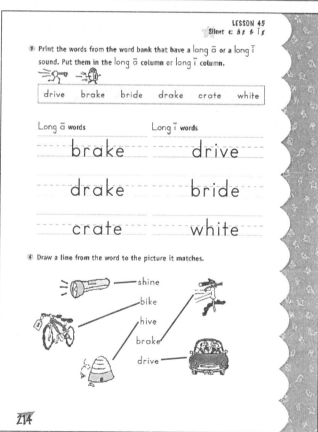

Activity 4. Review the pictures together. Have the student read the words and draw a line from the word to the picture it matches.

Pictures: **shine, brake, bike, hive, drive**

Activity 5. Read one word from each of the boxes. Student is to circle the correct word then print the circled words on the lines below.

Words: **time, tire, bride**
dime, brake, five
drake, fire, nine
hive, bake, lake

Activity 6. Use the white board to practice spelling. Teacher will write the beginning and ending sounds, leaving the vowel sound in the middle blank for the student to complete. Practice with several long **i** and long **a** words. When the concept is firm, have the student spell the words below the pictures by printing the correct long vowel sound.

Pictures/words: f**i**re, d**i**ve, h**i**ve
D**a**ve, s**a**le, dr**i**ve

Activity 7. Read the words in the word bank together and discuss the meaning of each. Read the sentences together and try the various words for each blank.

1. Dad will (**drive**) a mile.
2. Mike has a (**bike**) for sale.
3. Dave can fix a (**tire**).
4. Jake has a red and white (**cake**).

Activity 8. Have the student print and finish the sentence by printing his own name in the blank.

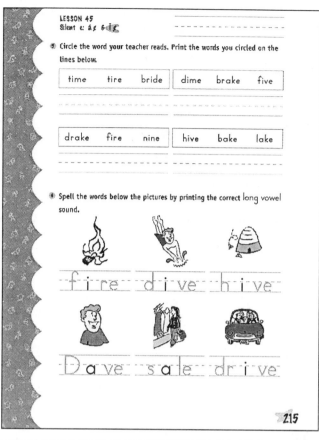

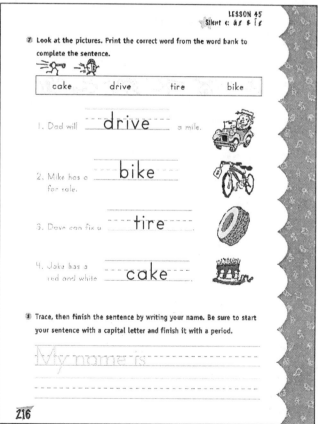

Lesson 46 - ck ending

Overview:

- Review Phonetic Rules
- Introduce the consonant **ck**
- Review rhyming words.
- Review alphabetical order

Materials and Supplies:

- Teacher's Guide & Student Workbook
- White board
- Alphabet flow-chart
- Reader 2: *Trix Does Tricks*

Teaching Tips:

When the consonants **ck** are together at the end of a word, it makes the sound of **k**. Demonstrate several words on the white board to illustrate the single sound of **ck**.

Activity 1. Review the Short Vowel Rule. Use the white board to illustrate the single sound of **ck** at the end of some words. Study the pictures together and discuss their meaning. Have the student put a circle around the pictures that have the sound of **k** at the end of the word.

Pictures: **kick, duck, black, fix**
lock, math, tack, clock

Activity 2. Use the white board to practice filling in the appropriate vowel. Teacher will write the beginning and ending sounds, leaving the vowel sound in the middle blank for the student to complete. Identify and discuss the pictures together. Have the student complete the word by printing the vowel in the word.

Words: st**i**ck, br**i**ck, d**u**ck
d**e**ck, bl**o**ck, s**i**ck

Activity 3. Read the sentences together. Have the student draw a line from the picture to match the sentence. Then the student will underline the words that end with **ck**.

Pictures: **Rick has a big check.**
The stick is in the can.
Dick can pick up the shells.
Jack has a rock in his sock.

Horizons Kindergarten Phonics

Activity 4. Read the words from the word bank together and discuss the rule for rhyming. The student will print the words from the word bank on the lines next to the word that rhymes with it.

sick/**Rick, Dick, kick**
luck/**buck, duck, tuck**
back/**sack, pack, rack**
neck/**deck, peck, check**
lock/**rock, dock, sock**

Activity 5. Use the alphabet flow-chart and puzzle to locate placement of words. Read the words to be alphabetized together. On the white board, print the letters in groups: [a, b, c, d]; [b, c, d, e, f, g, h, i, j, k, l, m, n, o, p, q, r, s]; [j, k, l, m, n, o, p, q, r]. Have the student locate the placement of each word under the alphabet letter. Then have the student print the words in alphabetical order in the workbook.

Words: **back   clock   Dick**
          buck   duck   sack
          Jack   neck   rock

Activity 6. Read the puzzle phrases together and discuss the pictures. Have the student draw a line from the phrase to the picture it matches.

Pictures: **Jack in a box**
          a pig with a pack
          a duck with a wig
          a fish can kick

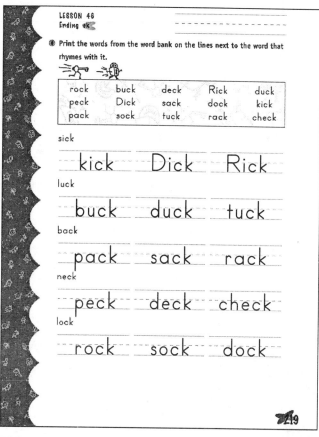

Activity 7. Read the words together. Have the student spell the words to match the pictures.

  Pictures: **duck, neck, sack**

Activity 8. Read the make-up words.

  Make-up Words: **dack, jick, teck, guck, yock**

Activity 9. Read the puzzle phrases together and discuss the pictures. Have the student draw a line from the phrase to the picture it matches.

  Pictures: **a flame on a hand**
  a flock of cats
  fan a flat
  flap the cloth

Activity 10. Read the sentence together and have the student copy it on the lines provided. Remind the student to begin the sentence with a capital letter and end it with a question mark.

Lesson 47 - Ending ing

Overview:

- Review Short Vowel Rule
- Introduce **ing** as part of a base word
- Introduce -**ing** as a suffix
- Answering direct questions

Materials and Supplies:

- Teacher's Guide & Student Workbook
- White board
- Reader 2: *Fishing*

Teaching Tips:

Introduce **ing** as part of a base word. Use the white board to demonstrate the initial consonant, then adding **ing** as a base word: **wing, thing, sing**.

Introduce -**ing** used as a suffix. By adding -**ing** to a word it means that it is happening NOW (present tense). Illustrate words: **camping, fishing, bumping, jumping**. Explain that sometimes the last consonant in a short word is doubled before adding the **ing**. On the white board demonstrate words as **sitting, dripping, clipping**.

Activity 1. The letters **ing** are word parts that are used at the end of many base words. Demonstrate the sound of **ing** as in **ring**. Read the words together. Have the student put a circle around the **ing** sound you hear at the end of the word for the pictures below.

Words/pictures: **ring, sing, wing, ding pink, bring, thing, fling**

Activity 2. The letters **ing** are word parts that are used at the end of many words to show that it is happening NOW. They make the same sound as above, but are used as a suffix. Study the words and pictures together. Have the student read the words alone and then put a circle around the **ing** sound you hear at the end of the word.

    Pictures: **sitting, mixing, hitting,**
               cutting, fixing, jogging,
               jumping, buzzing

Activity 3. Read one word from each of the boxes and have the student put a circle around the correct word in each box.

    Words: **fixing, rock, six**
            locking, Jack, box
            kick, kicking, take
            fish, ship, mending

Activity 4. Study the pictures, names of people, and question sentences. Have the student answer the questions by printing the name of the person on the line.

    Questions: Who is napping?   **(Jan)**
                  Who is milking?   **(Dad)**
                  Who is boxing?   **(Jack)**
                  Who is jogging?   **(Dick)**

Activity 5. Read the sentences together and discuss the pictures. Have the student draw a line to the picture that it matches. Underline the words that have the **ing** sound.

    Pictures: **Dad is hunting for a buck.**
               Jake is packing his sack.
               The cat is licking its leg.
               Rick is sitting on a bench.

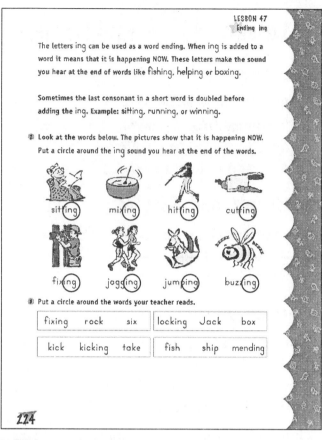

Activity 6. Read the word pairs together. Discuss that adding **ing** to the word shows it is happening NOW. Have the student print the words with the **ing** ending in the blanks in each sentence.

1. Dan is on a raft. Dan is (**rafting**).
2. Brad has trash to dump.
   Brad is (**dumping**) the trash.
3. Dave likes to box. Dave is (**boxing**).
4. Mom likes to mix a cake.
   Mom is (**mixing**) a cake.

Activity 7. Review the rhyming rules. Read the words in the word bank together. Have the student print the words from the word bank on the lines below the word that rhymes with it.

yelling/**telling**
jumping/**pumping**
hopping/**mopping**
fishing/**wishing**

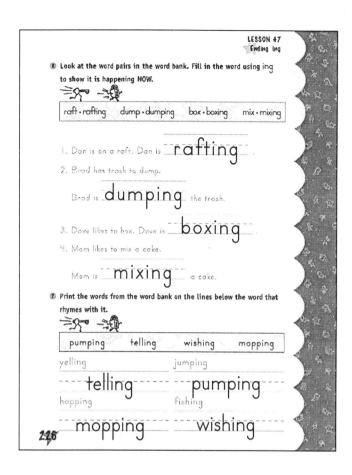

Lesson 48 - Review Long Vowels ā ¢ & ī ¢ Short Vowels

Overview:

- Review Short Vowel Rule
- Review Silent **e** Rule – ā ¢ and ī ¢
- Printing words to match pictures

Materials and Supplies:

- Teacher's Guide & Student Workbook
- White board
- Reader 2: *Jane's Cake*

Teaching Tips:

Review all the short vowel sounds. Review the silent **e** words: ā ¢ and ī ¢. Use of a picture to illustrate the meaning of a word.

Activity 1. Have the students name the pictures and put a circle around the ones that have a short vowel sound. Underline the short vowel.

> Pictures: **game, sand, fox, duck
> sun, mop, bat, dive**

Activity 2. Have the students name the pictures and put an **X** on the ones that DO NOT have a long vowel sound.

> Pictures: **Bible, dine, desk, fire
> pipe, milk, gate, pen**

Activity 3. Have the students name the pictures and draw a line from the word to the picture it matches.

> Pictures: **bike, fix, Jake, net, tub**

Activity 4. Read the make-up words.

> Make-up Words: **bame, dis, fam, sef, ket**

Activity 5. Have the student read the puzzle phrases. Discuss the meaning of each. Then the student will draw a line from the puzzle phrase to the picture it matches.

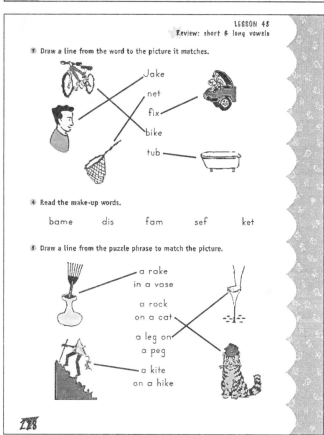

> Pictures: **a rake in a vase
> a leg on a peg
> a kite on a hike
> a rock on a cat**

Horizons Kindergarten Phonics

Activity 6. Read one word from each of the boxes. Student is to circle the correct word then print the circled words on the lines below.

Words: **fell, jell, sad**
kid, kite, Kate
made, game, like
wade, cut, wide

Activity 7. Write the words on the white board and have the student describe the meaning of each. Have him read the words in the word bank. Discuss the activity in each picture. The student will choose and print a word from the word bank that tells about the picture.

Pictures: **pen, game, dog, bake**

Activity 8. Have the student name the pictures. Then have him spell the word under each picture by filling in the vowel sound in each word.

Pictures: **r**o**ck, r**a**t, b**i**ke**
la**ke, r**i**b, v**a**n**

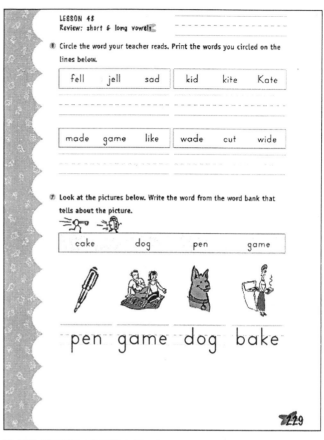

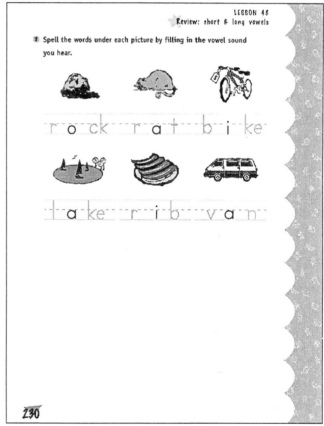

Lesson 49 - Silent e: ō é

Overview:

- Review long vowel sounds
- Review Phonetic Rules
- Review Silent **e** Rule
- Introduce silent **e**: ō é
- Compare short and long vowels
- Review rhyming words

Materials and Supplies:

- Teacher's Guide & Student Workbook
- White board
- Reader 2: *A Home for Old Rove*

Teaching Tips:

Introduce familiar word families with **o** and silent **e**: **one, ose, ome, ove, ode, ope**. Review the differences between short and long **o** sound in word change: **pop – pope, rob – robe**.

Activity 1. List vowels: **a, e, i, o**, and **u** on the white board with diacritical marking. Review the Silent **e** Rule. When two vowels are close together in a word, the FIRST one says its own name and the other one is silent, as in **bake, dine, rode, tune**. Use diacritical markings with a crossed out **e** and a straight line (macron) above the first vowel.

Study the pictures together and discuss the meanings for vocabulary development. Discuss family endings: **one, ose, ome, ove, ode, ope**. Have the student put a circle around the the pictures that have the long **o** sound.

Pictures: **bone, hose, rose, dome
rode, clap, rope, home**

Activity 2. On the white board print some three-letter words with short vowels. Have the student print an **e** at the end of the word and make the vowel change. Start with real words, then make-up words can be used in this learning exercise.

Study the pictures together and discuss the meanings. As soon as they understand the concept, have the student print the words with the short vowel **o**; then add a silent **e**. They will use diacritical marking to cross out the **e** and make a straight line over the long vowel **o**.

Words: **rod – rode, mop – mope**
pin – pine, rob – robe

Activity 3. Study the pictures and read the words together. Have the student draw a line from the word to the picture it matches.

Pictures: **hose, bone, drove, cone**

Activity 4. Study the pictures and discuss the meaning of each. Instruct the student to choose and circle the correct ending for the picture.

Pictures: r**ope**, r**ose**, n**ote**
h**ole**, w**ove**, ch**oke**

Activity 6. Read one word from each of the boxes. Have the students circle the correct word, then print the circled words.

Words: **dove, Dave, dive**
rope, rose, cape
cave, kite, home
dime, nose, line

Activity 6. Read the make-up words.

Make-up Words: **pome, loke, jove, bobe,**
goke

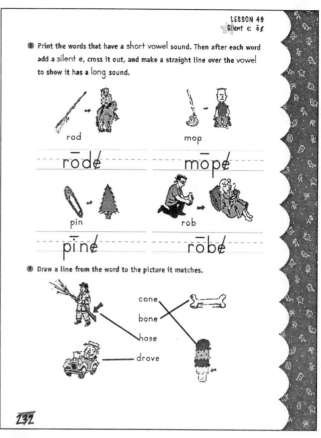

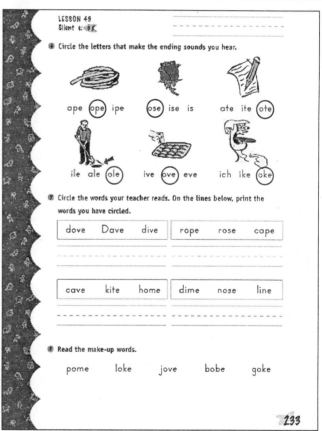

Activity 7. Read the sentences and words together and discuss the pictures. Have the student choose the correct word to finish the sentence and print it on the line.

Mom has a blue (**robe**).
Dave (**dove**) into the lake.
Blake (**rode**) his bike home.
The dog has a red (**nose**).

Activity 8. Review rhyming words. Have the student draw a line to match the words that rhyme.

Rhyming Words: **hole, pole, mole**
rose, hose, nose
poke, joke, choke
bone, tone, shone

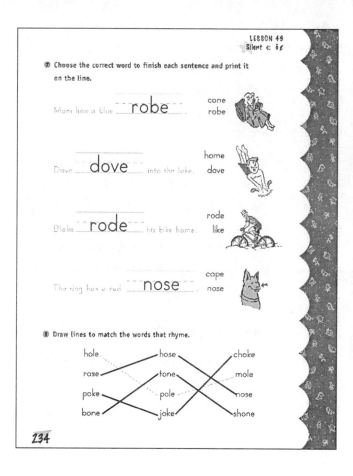

Lesson 50 - Consonant Blend gr

Overview:

- Review all long vowel sounds
- Review Phonetic Rules
- Review consonant blends that have been studied
- Word search
- Review alphabetical order
- Introduce consonant blend **gr**

Materials and Supplies:

- Teacher's Guide & Student Workbook
- White board
- Reader 2: *A Birthday Hike for Greg*

Teaching Tips:

Demonstrate the correct sound of **gr**. A picture of **grapes** can be used as an example of the sound. Use the white board to demonstrate the use of the blend **gr** with the vowels following.

Review the word search puzzle process by having the words printed on the white board and read aloud.

Activity 1. Review the Short Vowel Rules and the Silent **e** Rule. Use the white board to demonstrate the use of short vowels following **r**: **gra**, **gre**, **gri**, **gro**, **gru**. Indicate that the Silent **e** Rule is used as in **grave** or **gripe**. Study the pictures together to identify the beginning sound. Have the student put a circle around the pictures that START with the sound of **gr**.

Pictures: **Grace, branch, grove, grin grave, grass, grill, drake**

Activity 2. Use the white board to practice printing the blend with both capital **G** and lower-case **g**. Have the student practice printing **Gr** with a capital **G**.

Activity 3. Practice printing **gr** with lower-case letters.

Activity 4. Review the blends that have been studied so far. Identify the pictures and their beginning consonant blend. Have the student circle the letter under the picture that makes the beginning sound.

> Pictures: **gr**apes, **cl**amp, **cr**ust
> **fl**y, **Gr**ace, **gr**ab

Activity 5. Read the make-up words.

> Make-up Words: **grame, grap, gris, gred, grut**

Activity 6. Identify the pictures and read the words together. Have the student draw a line from the word to the picture it matches.

> Pictures: **flag, grape, grin, grill, drip**

Activity 7. Review alphabetical order. Use the alphabet flow-chart to help identify placement of words in alphabetical order. Print the letters on the white board: **c, d, e, f, g, h**. Have the student print the words in alphabetical order.

> Words: **crash, desk, flash, grass**

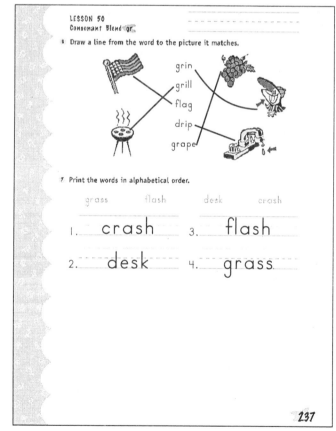

Activity 8. Read the puzzle phrases together and identify the pictures. Have the student draw a line from the puzzle phrase to the correct picture.

Pictures: **a grave in a box**
grass on the bed
a gray dog with red legs
grab a grill

Activity 9. Read the words that will be identified in the word search. Explain that words are hidden among other letters. Have the student circle the words that go across and down.

Across: **grab, drum, greet**
Down: **grand, gray, flake**

Activity 10. Read the sentences and the words from the word bank together. Discuss the answers that would be appropriate to complete the sentence. Have the students print the words on the line to make the sentence correct.

I like grass that is (**green**).
Did the dog (**grab**) the bone?
Grace has a (**gray**) cape.
We made camp in a (**grove**).

Activity 11. Identify each of the pictures and have the student print the beginning consonant blend for each word below the picture.

Pictures: **gr**een, **fl**ame, **gr**ab
Grace, **dr**ove, **gr**ave

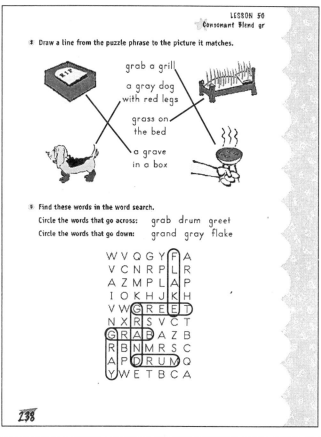

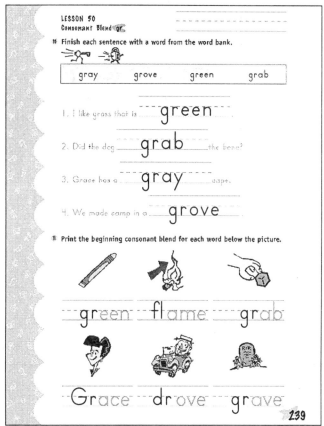

Activity 12. Read the sentence together. Discuss its meaning. Have the student practice printing on the white board. Then print the sentence in the workbook.

   Sentence: **Dad has a note for me.**

Activity 13. Give instructions. Teach color words.

Lesson 51 - Consonant Blend gl

Overview:

- Review long vowel sounds
- Review Phonetic Rules
- Review consonant blends that have been studied
- Review alphabetical order
- Introduce consonant blend **gl**

Materials and Supplies:

- Teacher's Guide & Student Workbook
- White board
- Reader 2: *Glen and the Sand Dollars*

Teaching Tips:

Demonstrate the correct sound of **gl**. A picture of **glue** or **globe** can be used as an example of the sound. Use the white board to demonstrate the use of the blend **gl** with the vowels following.

Activity 1. Review the Short Vowel Rules and the Silent **e** Rule. Use the white board to demonstrate the use of short vowels following **gl**: **gla, gle, gli, glo, glu**. Indicate that the Silent **e** Rule is used as in the word **glove**. Study the pictures together to identify the beginning sound. Have the student put a circle around the pictures that START with the sound of **gl**.

Pictures: **glad, Glen, glue, clam**
glove, grin, globe, glum

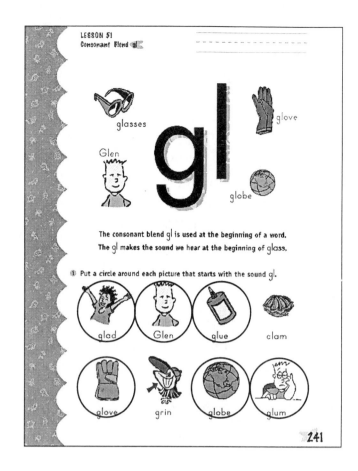

Activity 2. Use the white board to practice printing the blend with both capital **G** and lower-case **g**. Have the student practice printing **Gl** with a capital **G**.

Activity 3. Practice printing **gl** with lower-case letters.

Activity 4. Review the blends that have been studied so far. Identify the pictures and the beginning blends. Have the student circle the blend under the picture that makes the beginning sound.

> Pictures: **gl**ass, **gl**ue, **fr**og, **gr**ass
> **gl**obe, **fl**ash, **cr**oss, **cl**ip

Activity 5. Identify the pictures emphasizing the long vowel and silent **e** at the end of the word. Have the student circle the letters that make the ending sounds you hear.

> Pictures: gr**ove**, gl**obe**, dr**ake**, Gl**en**

Activity 6. Identify the pictures and read the words together. Have the student draw a line from the word to the picture it matches.

> Pictures: **cross, glove, glide, globe, grab**

Activity 7. Read one word from each of the boxes and have the student put a circle around the correct word in each box, then write the circled words on the lines below.

> Words: **globe, drove, clam**
> **Glen, Mike, Grace**
> **crime, gloss, grass**
> **brave, glue, grave**

Activity 8. Read the sentence together. Discuss its meaning. Have the student practice printing on the white board. Then print the sentence in the workbook.

> Sentence: **I am glad to be me.**

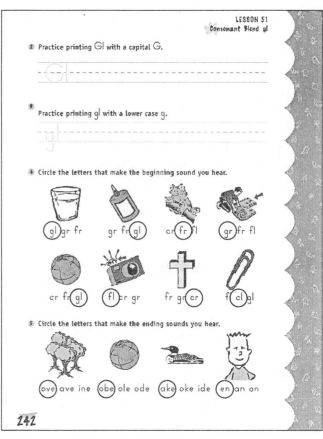

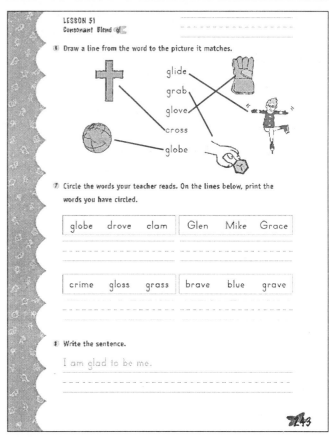

Activity 9. Use the alphabet flow-chart and puzzle to locate placement of words. Read the words to be alphabetized together. On the white board, print the letters with spaces between: **a, b, c, d, e, f, g**. Then have the student print the words in alphabetical order in the workbook.

Words: **apple, drink, elk, grove**

Activity 10. Read the sentences and words together. Discuss the appropriate word to use for a correct sentence. Have the student print the word on the blank.

Dan has a (**globe**) on his desk.
Glen is (**glad**) to be home.
Grace can hop on the (**grass**).
Dad had to fix the cot with (**glue**).

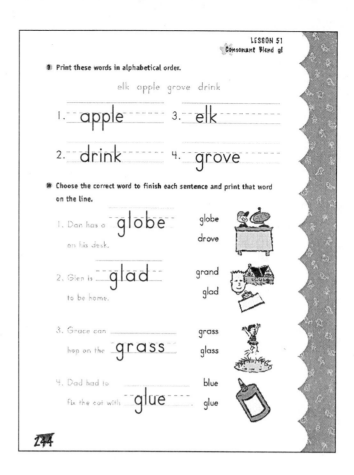

Lesson 52 - Consonant Blend sp

Overview:
- Review long vowel sounds and Silent **e** Rule
- Review Phonetic Rules
- Review consonant blends
- Introduce consonant blend **sp**

Materials and Supplies:
- Teacher's Guide & Student Workbook
- White board
- Reader 2: *Who Spilled the Milk?*

Teaching Tips:
Demonstrate the correct sound of **sp**. A picture of **spell** or **spade** can be used to illustrate the beginning sound. Use the white board to demonstrate the use of short vowels and words with silent **e** with the following beginning sounds: **spa, spe, spi, spe, spo, spu**.

Activity 1. Have the student put a circle around the pictures that start with the sound of **sp**.

Pictures: **spell, bell, spend, spool spade, spill, class, Spot**

Activity 2. Use the white board to practice printing the blend with both capital **S** and lower-case **s**. Have the student practice printing **sp** with a capital **S**.

Activity 3. Practice printing **sp** with lower-case letters.

Activity 4. Identify the pictures and read the words together. Have the student underline the beginning blend in each word.

Pictures: **Spot, spade, spill, spell, church**

Activity 5. Read the sentence together. Discuss its meaning. Have the student practice printing it on the white board. Then print

the sentence in the workbook.

Sentence: **I will spend my time at school.**

Activity 6. Identify the pictures and discuss the meaning of the words. Have the student put a circle around the pictures that end with **sp**. Underline the ending **sp**.

Pictures: chicken, cla**sp**, ship, ga**sp**

Activity 7. Study the pictures and read the words together. Have the student circle the **sp** that shows whether the **sp** is at the beginning or at the end of a word.

Pictures: **sp**end, wi**sp**, **Sp**ot, **sp**ell

Activity 8. Read the sentences together. Have the student draw a line from the picture to match the sentence.

Pictures: **A black spot is on the bench.**
Dad and Jake spend time at the lake.
Dan will clasp the fishing rod in his hands.
Beth tells Spot to spin.

Activity 9. Read the make-up words.

Make-up Words: **spof, fasp, spop, posp, risp**

Activity 10. Read the puzzle phrases together. Have the student draw a line from the puzzle phrase to the picture it matches.

Pictures: **a dog spent a dime**
spank a spot
spin a tire
spell on a sack

Activity 11. Identify the pictures together. Have the student spell the words below the picture by putting **sp** at the beginning or end of the word to make an appropriate word.

Pictures: **spank, grasp, spin, spend**

Lesson 53 - Consonant Digraph: tch, ch

Overview:

- Review short vowels
- Review consonant blends that have been studied
- Review crossword puzzles
- Introduce consonant digraph endings: **ch**, **tch**
- Exposure to word identification from definition for crossword puzzle

Materials and Supplies:

- Teacher's Guide & Student Workbook
- White board
- Reader 2: *The Chimps*

Teaching Tips:

Demonstrate the correct sound of **ch** and **tch** as used for wording endings. A picture of **lunch** and **catch** can be used as examples of the sound. Use the white board to demonstrate the use of the print examples of the sound.

Activity 1. Review the short vowels. Print words with short vowels on board and then substitute **ch** or **tch** for the ending. Study the pictures and words together. Have the student put a CIRCLE around the pictures that end with **ch**. UNDERLINE the words under the pictures that end with **tch**.

Pictures/Words: **catch, ranch, inch, bunch, ditch, patch, rich, lunch**

Horizons Kindergarten Phonics

Activity 2. Identify the pictures and read the words together. Have the student draw a line from the picture to the word it matches.

Pictures: **catch, pitch, hatch, match, inch, rich**

Activity 3. Read the words together and discuss word meanings for vocabulary development. Have the student read the words aloud. If a word ends with **ch** have him put a CIRCLE around the **ch**. UNDERLINE the **tch** if the word ends with those letters.

Words: **catch, munch, batch, Dutch, lunch finch, ditch, latch, patch, hatch**

Activity 4. Read the make-up words.

Make-up Words: **guch, litch, sach, metch, foch**

Activity 5. Read the sentence together. Have the student practice printing on the white board. Make note of the need for a capital letter at the beginning and a period at the end. Have the student print the sentence.

Sentence: **I had lunch with Dad.**

Activity 6. Read the puzzle phrases together. Have the student draw a line from the puzzle phrase to the picture it matches.

Pictures: **a ranch on an inch pinch a fish a sack on a match catch a glass**

Activity 7. Identify the pictures and discuss the meaning of the words. Use the white board to practice printing the beginning sounds to the word endings. When the concept is understood, have the student finish spelling the words under the pictures by filling in the beginning sounds.

Pictures: **lun**ch, **ha**tch, **in**ch **ran**ch, **ri**ch, **bun**ch

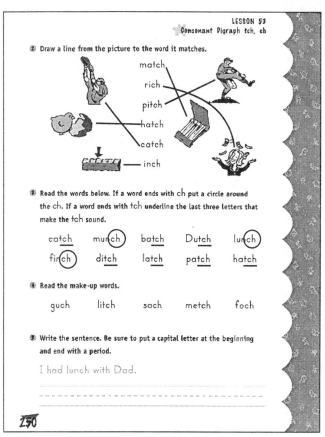

Activity 8. Read one word from each of the boxes and have the student UNDERLINE the correct word in each box. Then write the word on the lines below.

Words: **with, catch, past**
lunch, hitch, glue
inch, gasp, crash
pinch, shave, such

Activity 9. Discuss the definition of the word meanings with the student before they are exposed to the puzzle. Get several appropriate answers to increase their vocabulary. Use the white board to list possible answers. Work together with the student to complete the crossword puzzle.

Across: 2. It is your noontime meal.
(**lunch**)
3. Squeeze hard with your fingers.
(**pinch**)

Down: 1. A lot of things put together
(**bunch**)
3. Hit hard with your fist.
(**punch**)

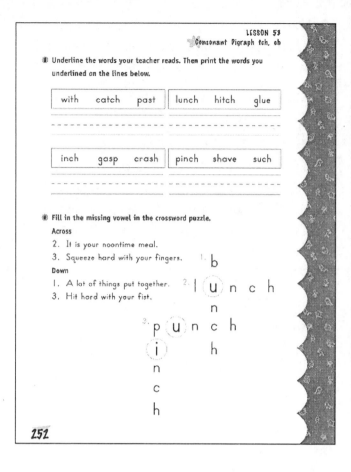

Lesson 54 - Review Short Vowels & Review Silent e: $\bar{a}$ é; $\bar{i}$ é; $\bar{o}$ é

Overview:

- Review silent **e**: $\bar{a}$¢, $\bar{i}$¢, $\bar{o}$¢
- Review short vowels
- Comprehension: Choice of sentences to match picture
- Review rhyming words

Materials and Supplies:

- Teacher's Guide & Student Workbook
- White board
- Reader 2: *Dopey's Home*

Teaching Tips:

Review the Vowel Rule and the Silent **e** Rule. Use the white board with a list of words with all of the short vowels. Have the student read the words. Then use the same words and have the student put a silent **e** on the word. Encourage him to pronounce the words, even though some may be make-up words. Use the white board to reinforce rhyming word activities.

Activity 1. Have the student read the words aloud. Then have him put a circle around the words that have a short **a** sound as in **pan**.

Words: **cap, map, sat, dip, brag, chin lid, bed, nap, kit, clap, flap**

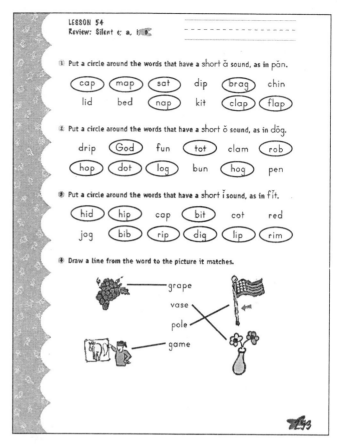

Activity 2. Have the student put a circle around the words that have a short **o** sound as in **dog**.

Words: **drip, God, fun, tot, clam, rob hop, dot, log, bun, hog, pen**

Activity 3. Put a circle around all the words that have short **i** sound, as in **fit**.

Words: **hid, hip, cap, bit, cot, red jog, bib, rip, dig, lip, rim**

Activity 4. Study the words and pictures together. Have the student draw a line from the word to the picture it matches.

Pictures: **grape, pole, game, vase**

Activity 5. Together with your student, review the words with short vowels. Student will put a silent **e** at the end of all the words and pronounce both sets of words. The student will mark the first vowel with a straight line, and cross out the silent **e**. Read the words again and put a circle around those that have a long **a** sound.

> Words: **cane, made, bite**
> **cape, time, fine**
> **dime, hope, robe**

Activity 6. Review the rhyming rules. Read the words in the word bank together. Have the student print the words from the word bank on the lines next to the word that rhymes with it.

> spank/**bank, drank, crank**
> spin/**thin, chin, win**
> spot/**dot, rot, hot**
> spill/**mill, fill, hill**

Activity 7. Read the words together. Student will put a silent **e** at the end of all the words and pronounce both sets of words. The student will mark the first vowel with a straight line, and cross out the silent **e**. Read the words again and put a circle around those that have a long **i** sound.

> Words: **tape, hide, rate**
> **pipe, kite, ride**
> **bite, code, fine**

Activity 8. Study the pictures together and read each set of sentences. Discuss the meaning for vocabulary development and comprehension. Have the student choose and underline the sentence that matches the picture.

> **Five men slip in the mud.**
> Five men sip punch.
> Jane has a game on the cot.
> **Sam will rest on the cot.**
> The dog has a big spoke.
> **The dog has a big bone.**
> **I like to ride a bike.**
> The milk is white.

64

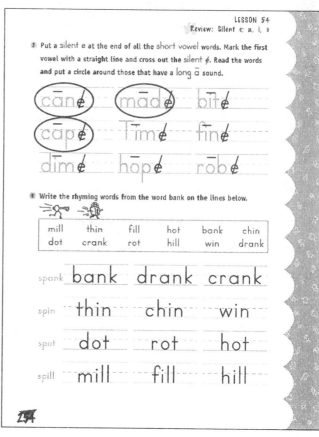

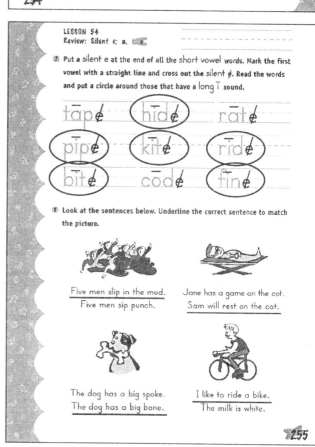

Activity 9. Together with the student, review the words with short vowels. Student will put a silent **e** at the end of all words and pronounce both sets of words. The student will mark the first vowel with a straight line and cross out the silent **e**. Read the words again and put a circle around the words that have a long **o** sound.

Words: **code, mope, pane**
pipe, hate, ripe
note, hope, robe

Activity 10. Read the words together and discuss their meaning. Student will print the long vowel words in separate columns.

Long **a** Words: **crane, fade, date**
Long **i** Words: **tire, side, mine**
Long **o** Words: **code, robe, note**

Activity 11. Review rhyming word formation. Discuss the word that would describe each picture. Then write the word for one of the pictures of each set of rhyming words on the white board. Encourage the student to locate the other picture that would make the words rhyme. The student could also dictate the spelling of some of the words. Make a game activity where the student becomes the teacher.

Pictures: **cane/mane**
dime/time
bone/cone
fish/dish
fan/can
dot/cot

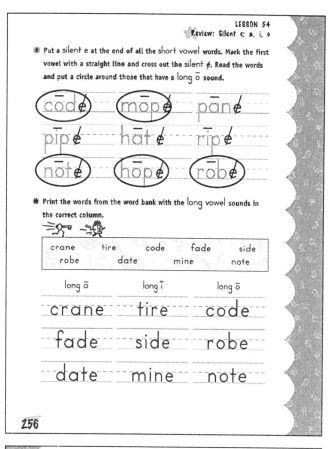

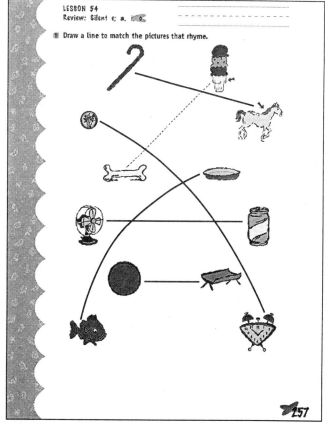

Activity 12. Color the picture. Give directions for colors.

Lesson 55 - Silent e: ū ¢

Overview:

- Review long vowel sounds
- Review Phonetic Rules
- Review Silent **e** Rule
- Introduce silent **e**: ū ¢

Materials and Supplies:

- Teacher's Guide & Student Workbook
- White board
- Reader 2: *Brute, the Mule*

Teaching Tips:

Introduce familiar word families with **u** and silent **e** on the white board with diacritical marking. Review the Silent **e** Rule. When two vowels are close together in a word, the FIRST one says its own name and the other one is silent as in: **flame, dime, pole, cute**.

Activity 1. Use diacritical marking with a crossed-out **e** and a straight line (macron) above the first vowel.

Pictures: **cube, fuse, tire, mule
clam, tube, flute, prune**

Activity 2. Study the pictures and read the words together and discuss the meanings. On the lines below, have the student print the words that match the pictures. Cross out the silent **e** and put a straight line over the vowel **u** to show it has the long **u** sound.

Pictures: **flute, mule, cube
dude, tune, June**

Activity 3. Read the make-up words.

Make-up Words: **clume, drise, flome,
grude, blaje**

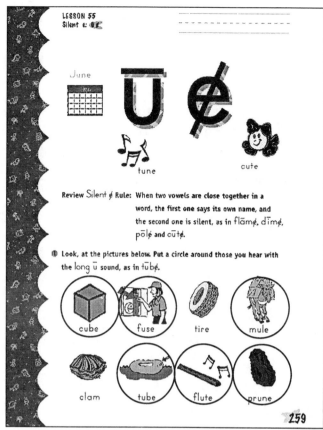

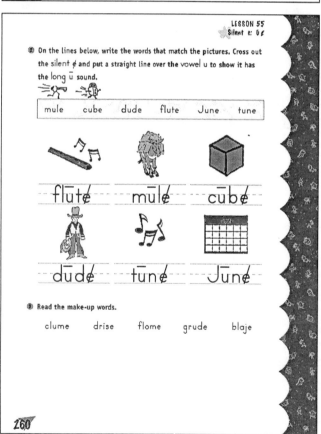

Activity 4. Read the sentences and words together. Discuss an appropriate word for each sentence. Have the student choose and print the correct word to fill in the blanks.

1. June is a (**cute**) girl.
2. The bad boy was (**rude**).
3. Put a (**cube**) of ice in the coke.
4. The big dog looks like a (**brute**).

Activity 5. Read one word from each of the boxes and have the student underline the correct word in each box.

Words: **cute, came, bun**
       side, mule, dike
       hand, June, ride
       tube, time, take
       camp, hand, tune

Activity 6. Read the puzzle phrases together and have the student draw a line from the puzzle phrase to the picture it matches.

Pictures: **Duke on a brute**
       a cute pig
       a cube with a fuse
       a mule with a flute

Activity 7. Identify the pictures. Have the student finish spelling the words by filling in the long vowel sound.

Pictures: m**u**le, c**u**be, m**o**le
       t**u**ne, m**i**le, b**o**ne

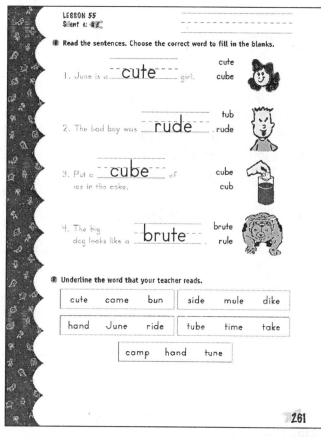

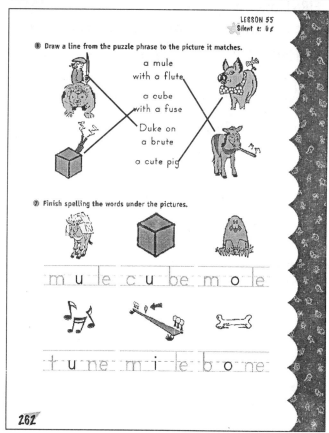

Lesson 56 - Review
Consonant Blends: bl, br, cl, cr, gl, gr, dr, fl, sp

Overview:

- Review consonant digraphs
- Review Phonetic Rules
- Review Silent **e** Rule
- Review consonant blends
- Review rhyming words from pictures

Material and Supplies:

- Teacher's Guide & Student Workbook
- White board
- Reader 2: *Brent, the Magic Man*

Teaching Tips:

Review all of the consonant digraphs and blends. Have the student print the beginning or ending sounds on the board as the teacher dictates. Reverse the process by having the student look at the printed sounds and tell the teacher what sound is made.

Activity 1. Review all the consonant blends and digraphs that have been studied. Study and discuss the pictures and their meaning for vocabulary development. Have the student put a circle around the pictures that begin with **bl** and a square around those that begin with **br**. On the lines below, print the beginning sounds to complete the spelling words that review **br** and **bl**.

Words: **bl**imp, **br**idge, **br**ush
　　　 brick, **bl**ink, **bl**ue
　　　 brake, **br**ead, **br**oke

Activity 2. Review **cl** and **cr**. Have the student put a circle around the pictures that begin with **cl** and a square around those that begin with **cr**. On the lines below, print the beginning sounds to complete the spelling words.

    Words: **cl**ip, **cr**ib, **cl**ock
            crate, **cl**ub, **cr**utch

Activity 3. Review **fl** and **dr**. Have the student put a circle around the pictures that begin with **fl** and a square around those that begin with **dr**. On the lines below, print the beginning sounds to complete the spelling words.

    Words: **fl**ag, **fl**ake, **dr**ess
            drum, **fl**ame, **dr**ip

Activity 4. Review **gl** and **gr**. Have the student put a circle around the pictures that begin with **gl** and a square around those that begin with **gr**. On the lines below, print the beginning sounds to complete the spelling words.

    Words: **gr**ass, **gr**in, **gl**ove
            globe, **gr**ill, **gl**ue

Activity 5. Read the words together. Discuss beginning and ending sounds. Have the student circle the correct **sp** to show whether the sound is at the beginning or at the end of the word.

    Pictures: ha**sp**, wa**sp**, **sp**ade, **sp**ell
               gra**sp**, **sp**ud, **sp**ill, cri**sp**

Activity 6. Read the words and the sentences. Have the student choose and print the appropriate word to make the sentence correct.

Nan had some (**glue**) to fix the book.
I had fun. I can (**grin**).
The top can (**spin**).
Tim can (**flip**) the dime in his hand.
The dog will (**drag**) the sock from the box.
The tot can (**clap**) his hands.

Activity 7. Review the formation of rhyming words. Have the student draw a line from the picture/words group to the picture that rhymes on the opposite side.

Pictures: **flame/tame**
          spade/blade
          brute/flute
          black/tack
          frank/tank
          clap/trap

Activity 8. Have the student print the sentence. Be sure to begin the sentence with a capital letter and end with a question mark.

Sentence: **Can the tot go to church?**

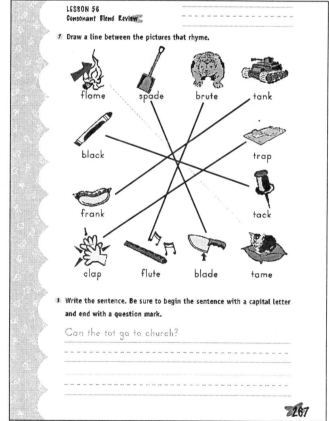

Activity 9. Have the student print the word with long vowel sounds in separate rows.

Long **a**: **grade, tape, Dave**
Long **o**: **lone, cone, dome**
Long **i**: **like, time, dive**
Long **u**: **tune, mule, cute**

Lesson 57 - Review Beginning Consonants & Blends

Overview:

- Review the alphabet letters and sounds
- Review Phonetic Rules
- Review Silent **e** Rule
- Review beginning consonant blends

Material and Supplies:

- Teacher's Guide & Student Workbook
- White board
- Reader 2: *Red Roses for Rose*

Teaching Tips:

Review all of the beginning single consonants and then the consonant blends. Have the student become aware of both beginning and ending sounds of the words. Use the white board to demonstrate as necessary.

Activity 1. Study the pictures together and discuss the meanings for vocabulary development. Have the student choose and circle the letter that makes the beginning sound you hear in each word.

Pictures: **fish, bake, gas, dig
gun, doll, box, fox
lunch, king, hog, jam
hand, jug, lock, kick**

Activity 2. Study the pictures together and discuss the meaning. Have the student choose and circle the letter that makes the beginning sound you hear in each word.

Pictures: **map, neck, quilt, net
queen, pack, mitt, pan
van, rack, sad, rat
sand, tag, vest, ten**

Activity 3. Study the pictures and discuss the meanings. Have the student choose and circle the consonant blend that makes the beginning sound you hear in each word.

Pictures: **glad, flag, clap, black**
class, flame, glass, Blake
crate, brake, grill, crush
brush, grove, drive, drake

Activity 4. Study the pictures and discuss the meanings. Have the student choose and circle the consonant blend or digraph that makes the beginning sound you hear in each word.

Pictures: **spud, chop, spot, ship**
thank, thin, chick, shot

Activity 5. Read the words and sentences together. Discuss the choice of words. Have the student choose the appropriate word to make the sentence correct. Student will print the word in the blank.

1. Ted has ten (**cats**).
2. Dick can sip the (**milk**).
3. Bob has lost his (**box**).

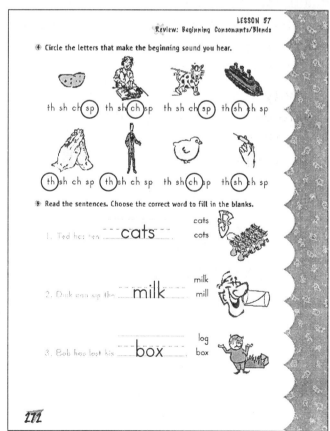

Lesson 58 - Consonant endings nd, nt & Nouns

Overview:

- Emphasis will be on ending sounds
- Introduce consonant ending sounds: **nd**, **nt**
- Introduce nouns as the name of a person, place or thing

Materials and Supplies:

- Teacher's Guide & Student Workbook
- White board
- Reader 2: *The Ant Hill*

Teaching Tips:

Review ending sounds. Introduce **nd** and **nt** used at the end of the word. Use the white board to demonstrate changing the single ending sound of word to a word using a blend. Introduce Nouns Rule: A noun names a person, place or thing. Stress that a person's name must have a capital letter at the beginning. Discussion will come later regarding noun used as a place.

Activity 1. Introduce the consonant ending **nd** and demonstrate the blended sound as in **hand**. Study the pictures together and discuss the meaning of each. Have the student put a circle around the pictures that have the sound of **nd** at the end of the word. Student will print the words that have been circled.

Pictures: **hand, fed, sand, bend**
mend, pond, fund, Ben

Activity 2. Introduce the consonant ending **nt** and demonstrate the blended sound as in **ant**. Study the pictures together and discuss the meaning of each. Have the student put a circle around the pictures that have the sound of **nt** at the end of the word. Student will print the words that have been circled.

> Pictures: **bent, mint, vent, hat**
> **tent, den, dent, hunt**

Activity 3. Read one word from each of the boxes and have the student put a circle around the correct word in each box.

> Words: **ant, band, bent**
> **tent, send, fond**
> **sand, land, dent**
> **mend, went, runt**

Activity 4. Study the pictures together. Discuss the words and the meaning. Have the student circle the correct ending—**nt** or **nd**—for each of the pictures below.

> Pictures: pla**nt**, sta**nd**, mi**nt**, po**nd**
> a**nt**, me**nd**, ba**nd**, hu**nt**

Activity 5. Introduce the Noun Rule. A noun names a person, place or thing. Discuss objects in the room that would be nouns. Talk about people's names and the use of capital letters for every name. (Proper nouns as places will be discussed later.) Study the pictures and read the names of people together. Have the student draw a line to the picture it matches.

> Pictures: **Dad, Beth, Dr. Tim, Mom**

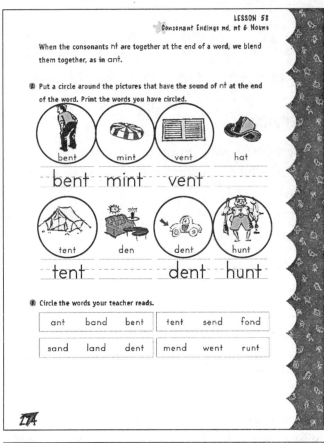

Activity 6. Discuss the pictures of things which are nouns. Study the pictures and read the words together. Discuss the words for vocabulary meaning. Have the student draw a line to the picture it matches.

Pictures: **horse, dog, swing, home**

Activity 7. Read the sentences together. Discuss the nouns that name a person. Have the student underline the noun that names a person and draw a line to the picture it matches.

Tom has a red car in the sand.
Jim can bend the wire.

Activity 8. Read the sentences together. Discuss the nouns that name a thing. Have the student circle the nouns that name a thing and draw a line to the picture it matches.

The pond is big.
Bill will send his dog to the tent.

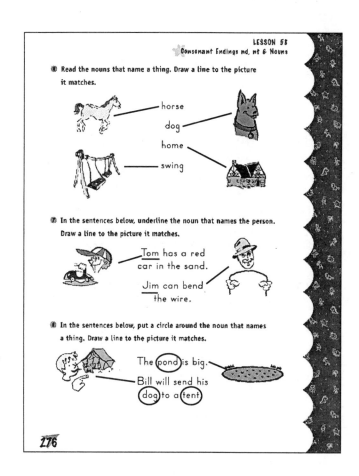

① Read the nouns that name a thing. Draw a line to the picture it matches.

horse
dog
home
swing

② In the sentences below, underline the noun that names the person. Draw a line to the picture it matches.

Tom has a red car in the sand.
Jim can bend the wire.

③ In the sentences below, put a circle around the noun that names a thing. Draw a line to the picture it matches.

The pond is big.
Bill will send his dog to a tent.

276

Lesson 59 - Consonant ending ng

Overview:

- Emphasis will be on ending sounds
- Introduce consonant ending sound **ng**
- Review of nouns

Material and Supplies:

- Teacher's Guide & Student Workbook
- White board
- Reader 2: *Ring the Bell*

Teaching Tips:

Review short vowel sounds. Introduce **ng** sound used at the end of the word. Use the white board to demonstrate changing the single sound of a word to a word using a blend. Example: **ran – rang**, **ten – tent**, **sing – sang/sung/song**. Review nouns as a name of a person or thing.

Activity 1. Study the pictures and read the words together. Have the student put a circle around the pictures that have the sound of **ng** at the end of the word. Then the student will print the words ending in **ng** that have been circled.

Words: **hang, rang, long, hand
lung, band, sang, gang**

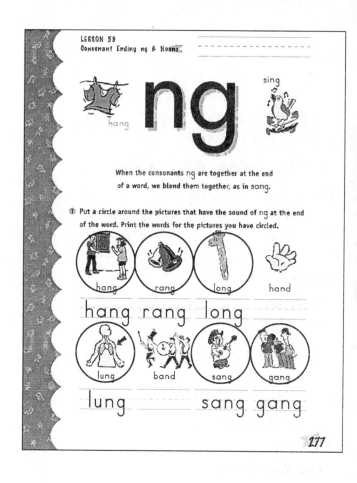

Activity 2. Study the pictures together and discuss the ending sound. Have the student put a circle around the correct ending for each picture.

Pictures: si**ng**, te**nt**, sa**nd**, lo**ng**
me**nd**, ba**ng**, ha**ng**, be**nd**

Activity 3. Review proper nouns: (nouns that name a person). Read the words together with the student. Make a note that the proper nouns will always have a capital letter. Have the student underline the nouns that name a person.

Words: **Brant, dog, Bob, cat, horse, Beth**

Activity 4. Review common nouns: (nouns that name a thing). Have the student underline the nouns that name a thing.

Words: **hand, Jim, song, tent, Jill**

Activity 5. Read one word from each of the boxes and have the student put a circle around the correct word in each box.

Words: **gang, sang, sand
band, ant, send
tent, hang, bend
lung, long, ring**

Activity 6. Read the sentences together. Discuss the meaning of the pictures. Have the student underline the correct sentence to match the picture. Put a circle around all the nouns that are names of persons.

The gang went to see the band.
Bob went to see the land.
Don had a hand in the pond.
Jan sang a song at the pond.
Dad sang the bell at church.
Dad rang the bell at church.
The ant was in a tent.
The mint was in a tent.

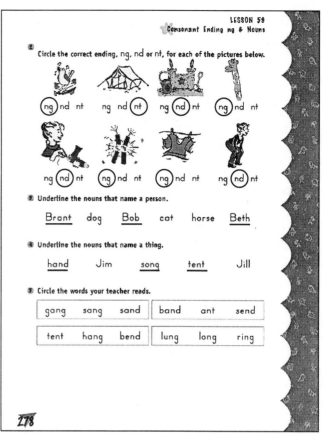

Activity 7. Find the pictures that rhyme with the following words.

  Pictures: **lung, gang, hand, tent, sang, band, bent, hang**

Activity 8. Read the sentence together. Have the student print the sentence on the lines below.

  Sentence: **I had fun when I sang a song.**

Activity 9. Read the sentences. Choose the correct word to fill in the blanks.

  1. The dog had a (**bone**).
  2. Mom can bake a big (**cake**).
  3. A clock can tell (**time**).
  4. It is hot in (**June**).
  5. Jon has fun in the (**tub**).

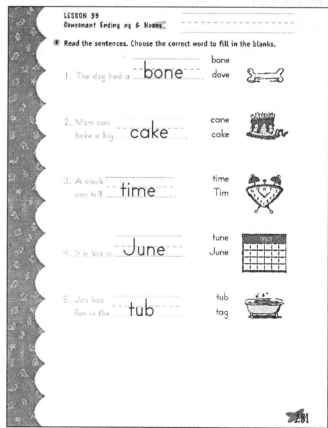

Activity 10. Look at the pictures and then choose a word from the word bank that tells about the picture.

1. Dad had a gun so he can get a buck. (**hunt**)
2. A black and red bug is in the sand. (**ant**)
3. Mom will fix my socks. (**mend**)
4. I can print with this. (**hand**)

Activity 11. Read the sentence with the student. Have the student print the sentence on the line below.

Sentence: **I like to grin.**

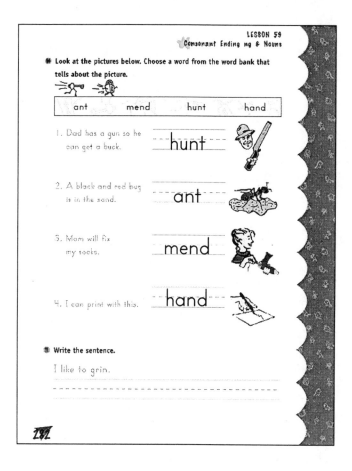

Lesson 60 - Consonant ending nk

Overview:

- Emphasis will be on ending sounds
- Introduce consonant ending sound **nk**
- Answering yes/no questions

Material and Supplies:

- Teacher's Guide & Student Workbook
- White board
- Reader 2: *A Skunk Can Stink*

Teaching Tips:

Review short vowel sounds. Introduce the **nk** sound used at the end of the word. Use the white board to demonstrate how changing word endings or a single letter will change the sound of the word. Example: **bank** – **bang** – **band**; **sink** – **sank** – **sunk**.

Activity 1. Study the pictures and read the words together. Have the student put a circle around the pictures that have the sound of **nk** at the end of the word.

Pictures: **bank, pink, sand, sink wink, Hank, junk, bent**

Activity 2. Let the student select and print five of the circled words ending with **nk**.

Activity 3. Study the pictures together and discuss the ending sounds of each word. Have the student put a circle around the correct ending for each picture.

Pictures: ga**ng**, ba**nk**, me**nd**, te**nt** a**nt**, bu**nk**, se**nd**, si**nk**

Activity 4. Read the words and sentences together. Have the student choose and print the correct word from the word bank to complete each sentence.

1. Dad had some (**junk**) in the tent.
2. Bill will get wet in the big (**tank**).

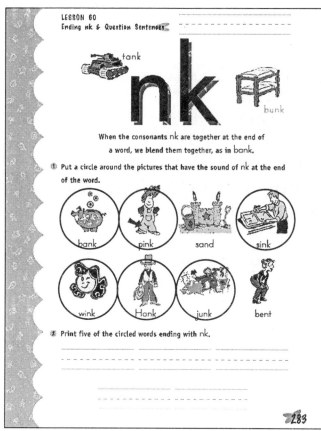

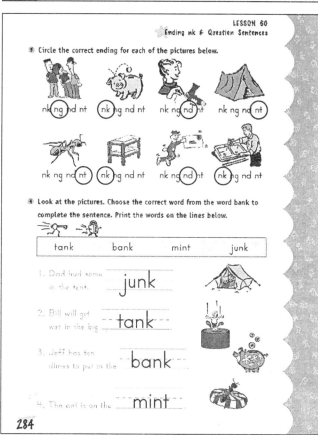

3. Jeff has ten dimes to put in the (**bank**).
4. The ant is on the (**mint**).

Activity 5. Read one word from each of the boxes and have the student put a circle around the correct word in each box.

Words: **bank, sang, mink, send**
hand, pond, ant, kink
bang, bent, Hank, mend
junk, rang, tent, lung

Activity 6. Review the formation of rhyming words. Have the student draw a line from the word group on the left to the words on the opposite side that rhyme. Stress that in most cases more than one word in the list on the right will rhyme with the word group on the left.

bank/**tank, Hank**
bunk/**junk**
hand/**band, sand, land**
sang/**gang, rang, bang, hang**
sent/**tent, bent, dent**

Activity 7. Identify and discuss the pictures. Read the question sentences together. Have the student circle **yes** or **no** to answer the question.

1. Is the runt pig in the pen? **yes**
2. Is the red ant on Bill's hand? **no**
3. Did Jim set up the tent yet? **no**
4. Did Hank ride in the van? **yes**
5. Can Jill wink? **yes**
6. Did the wind put a pile of sand in the path? **no**

Activity 8. Have the student choose one question sentence from above and print it on the lines. Be sure to use a capital letter for the first word and finish with a question mark (**?**).

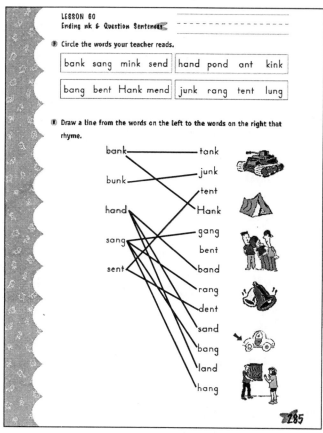

Lesson 61 - Review Ending Blends: ng, nk, nd, nt

Overview:

- Review Short Vowel Rule
- Review consonant blend endings: **ng, nk, nd, nt**
- Review proper and common nouns
- Alphabetical order

Material and Supplies:

- Teacher's Guide & Student Workbook
- White board
- Reader 2: *The Fun Hunt*

Teaching Tips:

Review the consonant blend endings: **ng, nk, nd**. Have the student print the beginning or ending sounds on the board as the teacher dictates. Reverse the process by having the student look at the printed sounds and tell the teacher what sound is made.

Activity 1. Study the pictures and discuss their meaning. Have the student put a circle around the words that end with the sound of **ng**, then print three of the words they have circled.

    Pictures: **gang, lung, slip, long**
                sang, rang, brag, fang

Activity 2. Read one word from each of the boxes and have the student put a circle around the correct word in each box. Then print the circled words on the lines below.

    Words: **gang, sang, land, sank**
             sink, wink, hunt, pond
             dent, hand, bend, mint
             think, blink, runt, lung

Activity 3. Study the pictures and discuss their meaning. Have the student put a circle around the words that end with the sound of **nk**. Print five of the circled words on the lines below.

Pictures: **bank, bent, mink, bunk junk, wink, sink, chin**

Activity 4. Review proper nouns. Have the student underline the nouns that name a person. Print only the names of the persons on the lines below.

Words: **Ted, sink, tent, Jim, Hank**

Activity 5. Study the pictures and discuss their meaning. Have the student put a circle around the words that end with the sound of **nd**. Instruct the student to print five of the words they have circled.

Words: **mend, hand, fix, bunk think, fund, bend, pond**

Activity 6. Review common nouns. Have the student underline the nouns that name a thing. Print only the names of the animals on the lines below.

Words: **tank, dog, band, hog, fox**

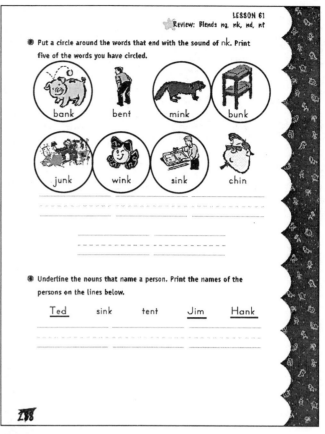

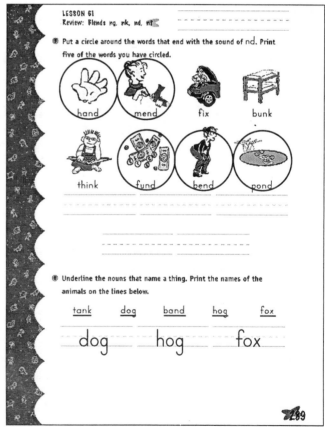

⑦ Put a circle around the words that end with the sound of nt. Print five of the words you have circled.

dent · tent · pond · hunt
vent · men · went · runt

290

⑧ Finish spelling the words under the pictures by filling in the ending sounds.

sink · tent · hunt
rang · bent · blink
mend · sang · gang

291

Activity 7. Study the pictures and discuss their meaning. Have the student put a circle around the words that end with the sound of **nt**. Print five of the circled words.

Words: **dent, tent, pond, hunt**
vent, men, went, runt

Activity 8. Have the student finish spelling the words under the pictures by filling in the ending sounds.

Pictures: si**nk**, te**nt**, hu**nt**
ra**ng**, be**nt**, bli**nk**
me**nd**, sa**ng**, ga**ng**

Activity 9. Use the alphabet flow-chart to locate placement of words. Read the words in each group together. On the white board, print the letter groups: **b,c,d,e,f,g,h**; **l,m,n,o,p,q,r**; **m,n,o,p,q,r,s,t**; **h,i,j,k,l,m**. Have the student locate the placement of the words for each group and print them in the workbook.

⑨ Print each row of words in alphabetical order.

hang gang rang bang

1. bang   3. hang
2. gang   4. rang

sink pink rink mink

1. mink   3. rink
2. pink   4. sink

mend send lend tend

1. lend   3. send
2. mend   4. tend

mint lint tint hint

1. hint   3. mint
2. lint   4. tint

292

Words: **bang, gang, hang, rang**
mink, pink, rink, sink
lend, mend, send, tend
hint, lint, mint, tint

Lesson 62 - Beginning Consonants: sc, sk

Overview:

- Review short vowel sounds
- Introduce consonant blends: **sc**, **sk**

Materials and Supplies:

- Teacher's Guide & Student Workbook
- White board
- Reader 2: *Scamp, the Treasure Hunter*

Teaching Tips:

Review short vowels. Demonstrate the sound of **sc** and **sk**. Stress that the sound is the same whether it is at the beginning or end of the word. Use the white board to illustrate **sc** and **sk** at the beginning with the short vowels.

Activity 1. Study the pictures and discuss their meanings. Have the student put a circle around each picture that starts with the letters and sound of **sc**. Print five of the circled words starting with **sc**.

> Pictures: **scooter, scalp, slide, scat Scott, scarf, scan, shack**

Activity 2. Study the pictures and discuss their meanings. Have the student put a circle around each picture that starts with the letters and sound of **sk**. Print five of the circled words starting with **sk**.

> Pictures: **church, skirt, skillet, skip skunk, drip, skull, skate**

Activity 3. Read one word from each of the boxes and have the student put a circle around the correct word in each box.

> Words: **skip, skit, clam skull, song, bank drink, skunk, sip shall, will, skill**

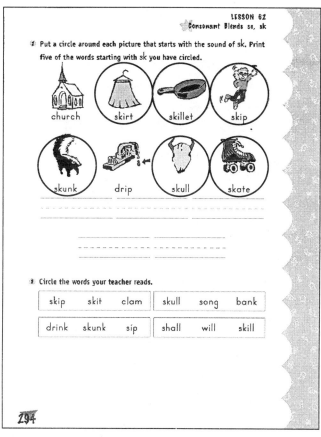

Activity 4. Read the sentences together. Discuss the meaning of each and compare it to the pictures. Have the student underline the correct sentence to match the picture.

Jack can skip on the path.
Jack can slip in the bed.
Dan can put on a skull.
Scott can run as fast as a skunk.
Don had a hole in his sock.
Bob cut the skin on his hand.
Will Meg get a red skirt?
Meg has a scab on her nose.

Activity 5. Review proper nouns. Read the sentences together. Have the student underline the noun that names the person. Draw a line to the picture it matches.

Pictures: **Jane saw a skunk at the lake.**
Did Meg scuff her shoe?
Scott can skip in the den.
Who has Jack's cap?

Activity 6. Read the words and sentences together. Discuss the words that would be appropriate to complete each sentence. Have the student choose and print a word from the word bank that tells about the picture.

1. Dick can (**sketch**) his mom.
2. The (**skunk**) ran up the path.
3. The red car will (**skid**) in the sand.
4. The (**skin**) on Jan's hand was wet.

Lesson 63 - Ending Consonant Blend sk

Overview:

- Review Short Vowel Rule
- Review ending blends: **nk, st, nt, nd**
- Introduce ending consonant blend **sk**
- Alphabetical order

Materials and Supplies:

- Teacher's Guide & Student Workbook
- White board
- Reader 2: *Fisk Has a Job*

Teaching Tips:

Review the short vowels. Demonstrate the sound of **sk**. Use the white board to illustrate **sk** at the end of short vowel words.

Activity 1. Study the pictures and discuss their meaning. Have the student put a circle around the pictures that have the sound of **sk** at the end. Print four of the circled words on the lines below.

Words: **mask, desk, bunk, dusk
task, list, flask, ask**

Activity 2. Study the pictures and discuss their meaning. Have the student put a circle around the correct ending for each picture.

Pictures: bru**sh**, de**sk**, a**sk**, ma**sk**

Activity 3. Study the pictures and discuss their meaning. Have the student put a circle around the correct beginning for each picture.

Pictures: **sk**unk, **sh**oulder, **th**ank, **sh**ip

Activity 4. Read one word from each of the boxes and have the student put a circle around the correct word in each box.

Words: **task, that, which
chat, bank, disk
skit, ask, back
Hank, band, sink**

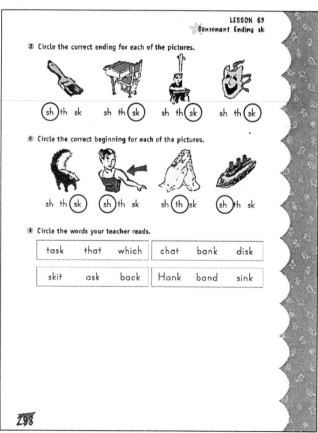

Activity 5. Study the pictures and discuss their meaning. Review the ending blend sounds on the white board. Have the student spell the words below the picture by printing the ending sounds.

   Pictures: ma**sk**, sku**nk**, chur**ch**
            tu**sk**, de**nt**, me**nd**

Activity 6. Read the words together. Have the student draw a line from the word to the picture it matches.

   Pictures: **disk, tusk, flask, husk, mask**

Activity 7. Read the sentences and study the pictures together. Have the student underline the correct sentence to match the pictures.

   Shad has on a mask.
   Shad has on a bask.
   Jill will ask Mom to go to the pond.
   Jill will flask Mom to go to the pond.
   Tad had a task to do in the den.
   Tad had a dusk to fix in the den.
   The elephant has a flask.
   The elephant has a long tusk.

Activity 8. Review rhyming. Study and discuss the pictures and their meaning. Have the student find the words that rhyme with the word/picture group. Draw a line from the word to the picture it matches.

   Rhyming Words: risk/**disk, brisk**
                  bask/**ask, mask, flask**
                  husk/**tusk**

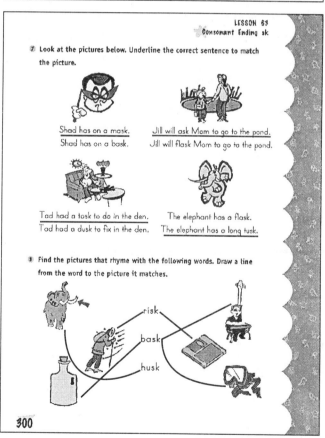

Activity 9. Read the words together. On the white board, print these groups of letters: **a,b,c,d,e,f,g,h,i,j,k,l,m,n,o,p,q,r,s,t; b,c,d,e,f,g,h,i,j,k,l,m,n,o,p,q,r,s;** and **b,c,d,e,f,g,h,i,j,k,l,m,n,o,p,q,r,s,t.** (Use the flow-chart to do the same thing.) Have the student locate the placement of each word under the alphabet letter. Then have the student print the words in alphabetical order in his workbook.

Words: **ask, bask, sank, task**
band, bank, hand, Hank
bent, dent, sand, tent

Activity 10. Instruct the student to connect the dots to make a picture and then color the picture.

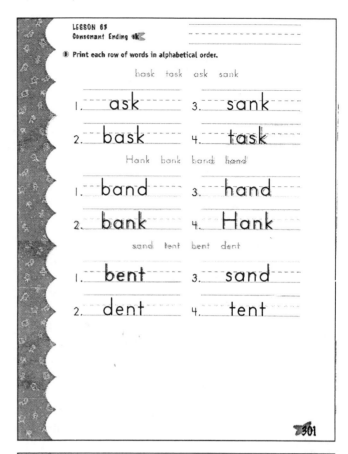

Lesson 64 - Ending Consonant Blend mp

Overview:

- Review short vowels
- Sentence construction and punctuation
- Introduce consonant ending **mp**
- Rhyming words

Materials and Supplies:

- Teacher's Guide & Student Workbook
- White board
- Reader 2: *Tramp*

Teaching Tips:

Review short vowels with the **mp** ending. Use the white board to illustrate the various sounds of the short vowel with **mp** endings. Use the white board to illustrate the kinds of sentences: telling, question, exclamation.

Activity 1. Study the pictures and discuss their meaning. Have the student put a circle around the correct ending for each picture. Print five of the words for the pictures that have been circled.

Pictures: **camp, pup, lamp, limp
tent, jump, pump, dump**

Activity 2. Study the pictures and discuss their meaning. Have the student circle the correct ending for each of the pictures below.

Pictures: hu**mp**, ju**mp**, lu**mp**, di**sk**
dri**nk**, du**mp**, me**nd**, pu**mp**

Activity 3. Review rhyming words and their formation. Read the words in the word bank together. Have the student print the rhyming word from the word bank on the lines.

camp/**ramp, damp, lamp**
rump/**lump, pump, jump**
wimp/**limp, gimp, blimp**

Activity 4. Review the sentence rule: A sentence is a complete thought that tells WHO DID WHAT. Every sentence must begin with a capital letter and end with a period (**.**), a question mark (**?**), or an exclamation mark (**!**). Read the sentences together. Have the student put an exclamation mark (**!**) at the end of each sentence. Then the student will choose one sentence with an exclamation mark to print on the lines below.

> **When I see a dump, I jump** [!]
> **Ouch, I hit my hand** [!]

Activity 5. Read the question sentences together. Have the student put a question mark (**?**) at the end of each sentence. Choose one question sentence to print on the lines below.

> **Can Meg go to camp** [?]
> **Will Dad fix the lamp** [?]

Activity 6. Read the sentences together. Have the student put a period [**.**] at the end of each sentence. Choose one sentence to print on the lines below.

> **We can go to the pump for a drink** [.]
> **Glen and Bob will romp in the den** [.]

Activity 7. Read one word from each of the boxes and have the student put a circle around the correct word in each box.

> Words: **pump, pup, punt**
> **limp, skunk, sip**
> **rang, camp, lung**
> **skip, scuff, lamp**

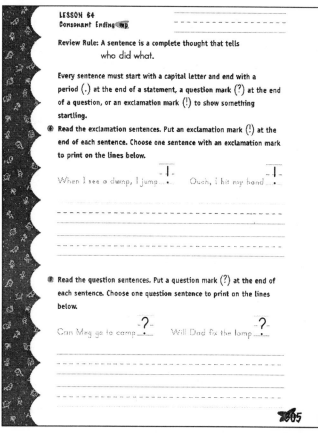

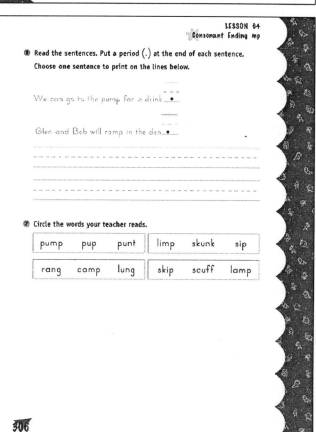

Lesson 65 - Consonant Ending lp

Overview:

- Review short vowels
- Introduce consonant ending **lp**
- Creative thinking – decisions
- Spelling

Materials and Supplies:

- Teacher's Guide & Student Workbook
- White board
- Reader 2: *Who Yelled for Help?*

Teaching Tips:

Review short vowels with the **lp** ending. Use the white board to illustrate the various sounds of the short vowel with -**alp**, -**elp**, and -**ulp** endings. Print the three words that end with **lp**.

Activity 1. Study the pictures and discuss their meaning. Have the student put a circle around each picture that ends with the sound of **lp**.

Pictures: **tusk, gulp, scalp, help bang, kelp, pulp, bent**

Activity 2. Study the pictures together and discuss their meaning. Have the student choose the correct ending for each picture.

Pictures: he**lp**, sca**lp**, ca**mp**, ma**sk** ta**sk**, di**sk**, ra**mp**, gu**lp**

Activity 3. Print all the words ending with **lp** on the lines below.

Words: **help, scalp, gulp**

Activity 4. Read the words together. Discuss activities the student enjoys doing. Have him put a circle around five things he likes to do.

Words: **skip, help, run, jump, jog skate, sing, clap, kick, bike**

Activity 5. Discuss sentence formation. Have the student choose the activity he enjoys. He will print the sentence and fill in the blanks

with two words of his choice.

Sentences: **I like to _____ and _____ the best when I have time.**

Activity 6. Read the sentences together. Have the student choose any two and print them on the lines below. Be sure to put a capital letter on the first word and a period at the end of the sentence.

Bill can ride his bike to camp.
Tom will help with the task.
Meg can gulp a drink.
Dad put his hand on his scalp.

Activity 7. Read the question sentences together. Have the student print any two of the question sentences on the lines below. Put a capital letter on the first word and a question mark at the end. Be sure to put a capital letter on the person's name.

What did Ben do to help Mom?
Did Sid wipe the dish with a rag?
Can Mike ring the bell?
Do you like white cake the best?

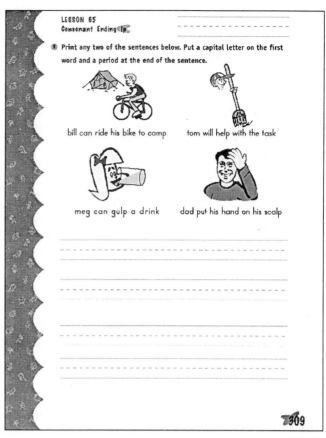

① Print any two of the sentences below. Put a capital letter on the first word and a period at the end of the sentence.

bill can ride his bike to camp   tom will help with the task

meg can gulp a drink   dad put his hand on his scalp

309

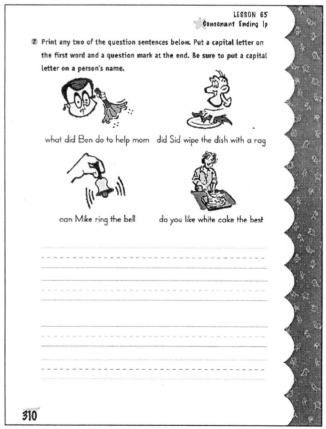

② Print any two of the question sentences below. Put a capital letter on the first word and a question mark at the end. Be sure to put a capital letter on a person's name.

what did Ben do to help mom   did Sid wipe the dish with a rag

can Mike ring the bell   do you like white cake the best

310

Activity 8. Study the pictures and discuss their meaning. Have the student spell the words below by printing the correct ending sound to complete each word.

Words: he**lp**, la**mp**, cra**sh**
    a**nt**, bra**nd**, pi**nk**

Activity 9. Read one word from each of the boxes and have the student put a circle around the correct word in each box.

Words: **scalp, crab, scab**
    yelp, crib, slip
    brand, help, crust
    skunk, song, skull

Activity 10. Color the picture by using the color key. Review color words.

Lesson 66 - Consonant ending lk

Overview:

- Review short vowels
- Introduce consonant ending **lk**
- Comprehension sentences
- Spelling
- Sentences with capitalization/punctuation

Materials and Supplies:

- Teacher's Guide & Student Workbook
- White board
- Reader 2: *Tim Gets Big*

Teaching Tips:

Review short vowels with the **lk** ending. Use the white board to illustrate the various sounds of the short vowel with: **elk, ilk, ulk**.

Activity 1. Study the pictures and discuss their meaning. Have the student put a circle around the pictures that have the sound of **lk** at the end of the word.

Pictures: **milk, silk, skip, sulk**
bulk, hulk, skit, sick

Activity 2. Read the sentences and the words in the word bank together. Discuss the meaning to check comprehension. Have the student spell the word from **Activity 1** that tells about each sentence:

Spell the word if you want to drink something white. (**milk**)
Spell the word if you feel like a grump. (**sulk**)
Spell the word when you feel soft cloth on your skin. (**silk**)
Spell the word if you see someone big and strong. (**hulk**)

Activity 3. Read the words together. Have the student draw a line from the word to the picture it matches.

Pictures: **sulk, milk, disk, hulk**

Activity 4. Read one word from each of the

boxes and have the student circle the correct word in each box.

Words: **hulk, hump, had / line, silk, mask**
dusk, milk, ask / bulk, dusk, task

Activity 5. Study the pictures and discuss their meaning. Have the student spell the word below the picture by printing the ending sound.

Pictures: mi**lk**, la**mp**, he**lp**
ha**nd**, lo**ng**, ba**nk**

Activity 6. Read the sentences together. Discuss the pictures. Have the student underline the correct sentence to match the picture.

Jan has a silk dress.
Jan has a skip dress.
Jack has a hat on the list.
Jack is mad and will sulk.

Activity 7. Read the sentences together. Discuss the need for capital letters at the beginning of the sentence and for a person's name. Use the correct punctuation for the end of the sentence. Have the student print the sentences on the lines below.

Did Peg drink the milk?
Can Jan get a silk dress?
Tom went to the camp.
Will you print your name?

Lesson 67 - Review
endings: sk, mp, lp, lk, ng, nk, nd, nt

Overview:

- Review consonant endings: **sk, mp, lp, lk, ng, nt, nd, nt**
- Spelling
- Alphabetical order

Materials and Supplies:

- Teacher's Guide & Student Workbook
- White board
- Alphabet flow-chart
- Reader 2: *Hank, the Jester*

Teaching Tips:

Review consonant endings: **sk, mp, lp, lk ng, nk, nd, nt**. Use the white board to illustrate the various sounds of the short vowel with the endings.

Activity 1. Study the pictures and discuss their meanings. Have the student circle the letters that make the correct ending sound.

Pictures: ri**ng**, Ha**nk**, ba**nd**, te**nt**

Activity 2. Study the pictures and discuss their meaning. Have the student circle the letters that make the correct ending sound.

Pictures: gu**lp**, mi**lk**, ca**mp**, whi**sk**

Activity 3. Study the pictures together. Have the student spell the words under each picture.

Pictures: **lamp, jump, dump**

Activity 4. Study the pictures and discuss the meaning. Have the student print the letters that make the correct ending sound for each word under the picture.

Pictures: ca**mp**, gu**lp**, tu**sk**
scal**lp**, mi**lk**, ma**sk**

Horizons Kindergarten Phonics

Activity 5. Study the pictures together. Have the student spell the words under each picture.

Pictures: **hunt, band, gang**

Activity 6. Use the alphabet flow-chart to locate placement of words. Read the words to be alphabetized together. On the white board, print the letters for each word in groups: **b,c,d,e,f,g,h,i,j**;
f,g,h,i,j,k,l,m,n,o,p,q,r,s,t,u,v,w;
a,b,c,d,e,f,g,h,i,j,k,l,m;
b,c,d,e,f,g,h,i,j,k

Have the student locate the placement of each word under the alphabet letter. Then have the student print the words in alphabetical order in the workbook.

Words: **bent, Bill, clap, fund**
Jan, junk, men, vent
ant, band, Kent, wink

Activity 7. Read the sentences and the words in the word bank. Have the student choose the appropriate word to print in the sentence.

1. Jan has a (**pink**) dress.
2. Bob (**sang**) a song.
3. Mom put a glass of (**milk**) on the stand.
4. Put your (**hand**) on the dog.
5. I can (**help**) Dad in the den.
6. The cat has a big (**fang**).

Activity 8. Read the sentences together. Discuss the pictures. Have the student underline the correct sentence to match the picture.

Brad will drink the sink.
Brad will drink the milk.
Sam is a hulk of a man.
Sam can hand the man a cap.

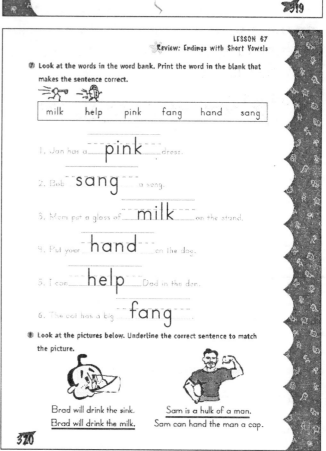

Horizons Kindergarten Phonics

Lesson 68 - Review
Beginning Consonant Blends

Overview:

- Review consonant blend beginnings
- Review Silent **e** Rule
- Review Short Vowel Rule
- Alphabetical order
- Spelling
- Rhyming words

Materials and Supplies:

- Teacher's Guide & Student Workbook
- Alphabet flow-chart
- White board
- Reader 2: *Stan's Big Pants*

Teaching Tips:

Review the beginning consonant blends. Use the white board to illustrate the various beginnings used with short and long vowels. Review Short and Long Vowel Rules.

Activity 1. Study the pictures and discuss their meaning. Have the student circle the letters that make the beginning sound you hear.

Pictures: **bl**ack, **cr**ab, **cl**am, **bl**ue **br**and, **cl**ip, **cr**ib, **cr**utch

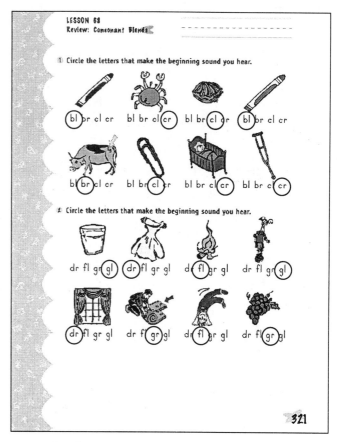

Activity 2. Study the pictures and discuss their meaning. Have the student circle the letters that make the beginning sound you hear.

Pictures: **gl**ass, **dr**ess, **fl**ame, **gl**ide **dr**ape, **gr**ass, **fl**ip, **gr**ape

Activity 3. Study the pictures and discuss their meaning. Have the student circle **sk** to show if it is at the beginning or the end of the word.

Pictures: **sk**ip, di**sk**, **sk**unk, ma**sk**
skull, **sk**illet, de**sk**, **sk**id

Activity 4. Read the words together. Use each group of words independently. Have the student draw a line from the words in each column that rhyme.

crab/grab
clip/slip
grin/fin
glue/blue
clam/slam
crib/rib
grape/tape
dress/bless
disk/risk
dusk/husk

Activity 5. Study the pictures together. Have the student spell the words by filling in the beginning blends.

Pictures: **bl**imp, **gl**ue, **sp**ank
clock, **fl**ag, **sp**in
brick, **gr**ass, **gl**ove
crate, **dr**um, **br**ake

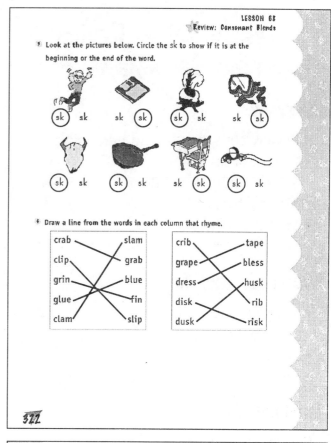

Activity 6. Read the words and sentences together. Have the student choose the appropriate word to print in the sentence.

1. Dad will dig it with a (**spade**).
2. Jim can (**spend**) his dimes for a cap.
3. Jack put the (**glove**) on his hand.
4. Jan had to (**glue**) the rug to fix it.
5. I like to see you (**grin**).
6. Did Mom put a (**dress**) on the doll?

Activity 7. Read one word from each of the boxes and have the student put a circle around the correct word in each box.

Words: **sink, gang, bent**
band, dent, disk
wimp, hemp, brag
hand, vent, long
scalp, sent, think
sand, rang, lung
milk, long, sent
junk, pink, fang

Activity 8. Study the pictures together. Have the student print the letters that make the correct ending sound for each word.

Pictures: fa**ng**, ju**nk**, be**nt**
me**nd**, sa**nd**, pi**nk**

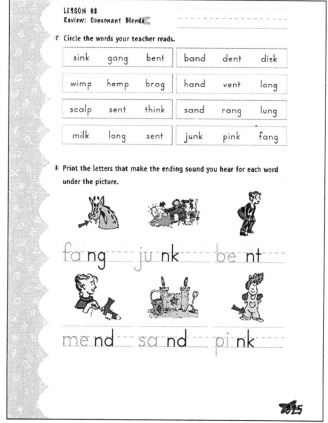

Activity 9. Use the alphabet flow-chart to locate placement of words. Read the words together.

Words: **flag, glad, spank**

Activity 10. Use the alphabetical flow-chart to locate placement of words. Read the words together.

Words: **flake, glue, help**

Activity 11. Read the sentence together. Have the student print it on the lines below.

Sentence: **I bless and thank God all the time.**

Lesson 69 - Consonant Blend pl & Pronouns

Overview:

- Review short and long vowels
- Introduce consonant blend **pl**
- Introduce pronouns
- Changing nouns to pronouns

Materials and Supplies:

- Teacher's Guide & Student Workbook
- White board
- Reader 2: *Planting Time*

Teaching Tips:

Review the short and long vowels. Use the white board to illustrate the consonant blend **pl** with the vowels. Review nouns. Introduce pronouns. Use discussion and the white board to illustrate the substitution of a pronoun for a noun. Have the students become familiar with all the pronouns listed.

Activity 1. Study the pictures and discuss the sound of **pl** at the beginning of the pictures. Check the vocabulary meaning for each. Have the student put a circle around the pictures that start with the sound **pl**.

Pictures: **plant, planet, clamp, plank rat, plum, play, plate**

Activity 2 & 3. Have the student practice printing **Pl** with a capital **P** and with lowercase letters.

Activity 4. Review the beginning blends: **pl, gl, cl**. Study the pictures and discuss their meaning. Have the student put a circle around the correct beginning blend.

Pictures: **pl**ant, **gl**ad, **cl**amp, **pl**us **gl**ide, **pl**um, **pl**ug, **cl**ump

Activity 5. Read the words together. Use the alphabet flow-chart to locate the beginning sound for alphabetizing. Print the sequence of letters to have the student find the place-

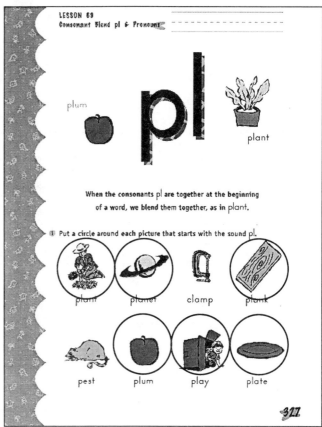

ment of words for each set. Have the student print the words in alphabetical order.

Words: **drum, plug, sick**

Activity 6. Read the words together and discuss the meaning of the pictures. Have the student draw a line from the word to the picture it matches.

Pictures: **drum, plus, plank, plug, planet**

Review the Noun Rule: Discuss the names of people and the need for capitalization. Review common nouns that do not require the use of a capital letter.

Introduce the Pronoun Rule: A pronoun can take the place of a noun. A pronoun doesn't need a capital letter (except for the pronoun **I** unless it is used at the beginning of the sentence. Use the white board print some proper nouns. Have the student choose a pronoun that could replace a noun:

he:	Bob	**they**:	Jack and Sam
she:	Nan	**I**:	student's name
him:	Jim	**us**:	student's name and Dan
his:	Don	**me**:	student's name
her:	Fran	**you**:	teacher's name
we:	student's name and someone else.		

Activity 7. Learn to read the pronouns in the word bank.

Words: **I, he, she, you, me, they, him, her, his**

Activity 8. Have the student print the sentence and underline the pronoun.

Sentence: **I am happy.**

Activity 9. Read the words and sentences. Discuss substituting pronouns for nouns. Have the student change the noun to a pronoun. Print the pronoun on the lines below.

1. (**He**) lost the plug for his van.
2. (**She**) can sit on the plank.
3. (**I**) like to print.
4. Tom gave the plum to (**me**).
5. (**They**) can drive a van.
6. The dog can go home with (**him**).
   It is (**his**) dog.
7. The cat can rest on the cot with (**her**).

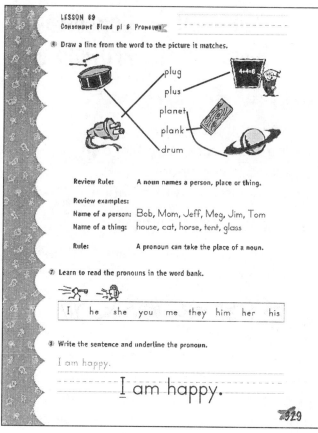

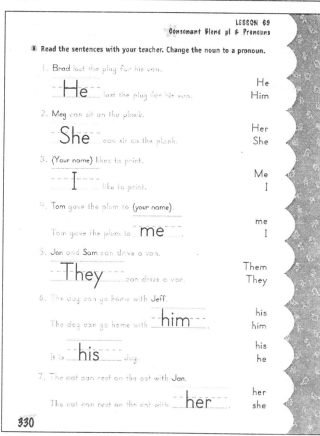

Lesson 70 - Review: Beginning Consonant Blends

Overview:
- Review beginning consonant blends
- Review nouns and pronouns
- Create sentences from personal wish

Materials and Supplies:
- Teacher's Guide & Student Workbook
- White board
- Reader 2: *Spud Does Tricks*

Teaching Tips:
Use the white board to review beginning and ending consonant blends. Encourage conversation indicating sentence structure.

Activity 1. Review the consonant blends at the beginning of words. Have the student circle the letters that make the beginning sounds you hear. Print two of the words that begin with **br**.

Pictures: **br**ide, **dr**ip, **fl**ap, **cl**own
flash, **br**ake, **dr**ess, **cl**am

Activity 2. Read the sentences together. Review the rule for pronouns. Have the student underline the pronouns in the sentences below.

She has a blue dress.
He can go to the lake.
They will get to run up the path.
Will you sing a song?
I like to camp.
Buff is his dog.

Activity 3. Have the student circle the letters that make the beginning sounds you hear. Print two of the words that begin with **gl**.

Pictures: **cr**ab, **gr**ass, **gl**ass, **fl**ag
flip, **gr**ape, **gl**ad, **cr**ib

Activity 4. Have the student circle the letters that make the beginning sound you hear. Print two of the words that begin with **ch**.

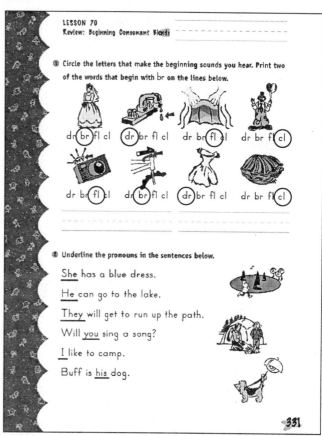

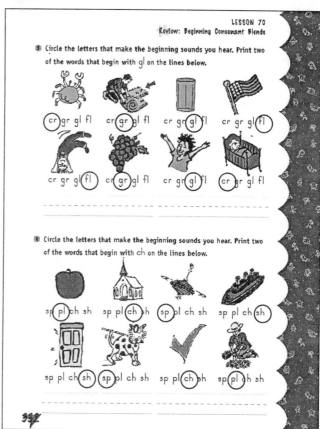

Pictures: **pl**um, **ch**urch, **sp**in, **sh**ip
shut, **Sp**ot, **ch**eck, **pl**ant

Activity 5. Review the Noun Rule. Have the student underline the nouns in the sentences below.

**The dog and the cat sat in the tent.
Jeff and Ned can go to camp.**

Activity 6. Have the students print the nouns. Discuss which are the names of persons (proper nouns) and which are the names of things (common nouns).

Words: **dog, cat, tent, Jeff, Ned**

Activity 7. Have the student print the pronouns in the word bank on the lines below.

Words: **she, he, they, you, I, his**

Activity 8. Discuss sentences again. Have the student make up and dictate to the teacher a sentence using the pronoun "I". Start with: "I like to...." Teacher will write it on the white board and have the student copy it in his workbook.

Activity 9. Draw a picture of what you like to do.

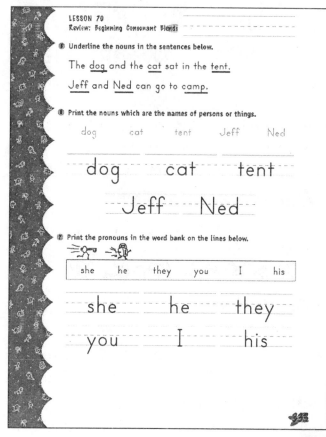

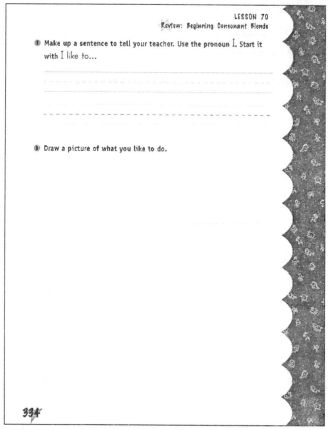

Lesson 71 - Double Vowels: ai

Overview:

- Review names of vowels used as long vowel sounds
- Introduction of double vowels: **ai**
- Comprehension choice of words

Materials and Supplies:

- Teacher's Guide & Student Workbook
- White board
- Reader 2: *A Train Ride*

Teaching Tips:

Teach the Double Vowel Rule: When two vowels are close together in a word, the first one is long (says its own name) and the second one is silent.

Use the white board to demonstrate the change the short vowel sound of **a** to a long **a**. Experiment with a list of words with short **a** sound, then adding the letter **i** after it. Example: **pan – pain; man – main; lad – laid; pal – pail.**

Use the technique of crossing out the second vowel and putting a straight line over the first vowel.

Activity 1. List vowels **a, e, i, o, u** on the white board. The student must be aware that the name of the letter is the same as the long sound. Study the pictures together and discuss the vocabulary meaning. Be sure the student is aware of the long **a** sound in the middle of the word. Have the student circle the picture with the double vowel for the sound that matches.

Pictures: bat, **Gail, mail, jail
pail**, fan, **rain, hair**

Activity 2. Study the pictures together. On the white board print the words and have the student cross out the second vowel and make a straight line over the first vowel to show that it has a long sound. Have the student read the words under the pictures and print them on the lines below.

Pictures: **pail, pain, quail, sail, faith**

Activity 3. Study the pictures and draw a line from the word to match the picture.

Pictures: **sail, paint, nail, tail, bait.**

Activity 4. Read the words together. Review the rhyming process, noting that all the words end in the same sound. Have the student print four of the words from the word bank that rhyme with the word **Gail**.

Words: **tail, sail, nail, rail, mail**

Activity 5. Print the words on the white board and have the student cross out the second vowel and put a straight line over the first vowel. Student will read the make-up words.

Make-up Words: **naid, shaib, gaid, laif, plaip, blaig**

Activity 6. Read the puzzle phrases together. Have the student draw a line from the puzzle phrase to the picture it matches.

Pictures: **hair in a pail**
a tail on Gail
paint the quail
a nail with bait

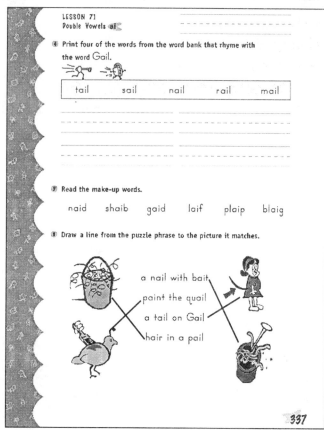

Activity 7. Read the words and the sentences together. Have the student experiment with each word choice and decide which one would be an appropriate answer. When a selection is made, have him print the word on the line.

1. Gail ran to get the (**mail**).
2. Jane had a (**pail**) of rain water.
3. The hen (**laid**) ten eggs in the nest.
4. We (**paid**) the maid ten dimes.
5. Sam put the (**bait**) on the fish line.

Activity 8. Read the sentence together. Have the student print the sentence on the lines below.

Sentence: **I have faith in God.**

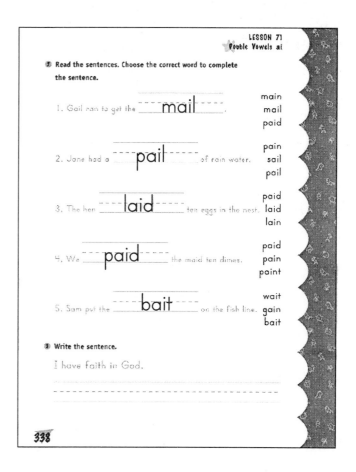

Lesson 72 - Consonant Blend with ai

Overview:

- Review names of vowels used as long vowel sounds
- Double vowels **ai** used with consonant blends
- Comprehension – choice of words in sentences

Materials and Supplies:

- Teacher's Guide & Student Workbook
- Alphabet flow-chart
- White board
- Reader 2: *The Snail Trail*

Teaching Tools:

Review Double Vowel Rule. Use the white board to demonstrate the use of consonant blends at the beginning of a word followed by **ai**.

Activity 1. Read the words under the pictures together. Identify the pictures and discuss the meaning. Review the sound **ai** makes in a word. Demonstrate on the white board by crossing out the second vowel and putting a straight line over the first vowel. Have the student put a circle around the pictures that have the long **a** sound.

Pictures/words: **train, snail, chain, stain brain, grain, trail, quail**

Activity 2. Have the student print three of the words above that end with **ain**.

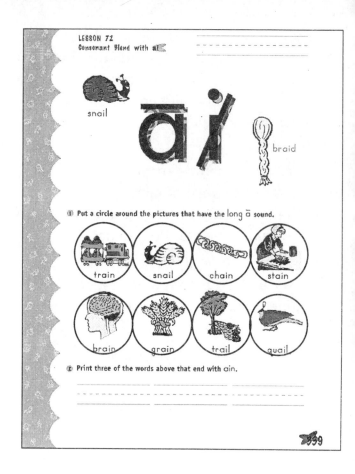

Horizons Kindergarten Phonics

Activity 3. Have the student print two of the words in **Activity 1** that begin with the consonant blend **tr**.

Activity 4. Have the student print the word that is the name of a bird.

Activity 5. Study the pictures and discuss the meaning. Have the student put a circle around the pictures that have the long **a** sound. Mark an **x** on those that have a short vowel sound.

 Pictures: **bait, pet, sail, ran**
  stand, rain, sell, Spot

Activity 6. Read the make-up words together.

 Make-up Words: **chaim, braif, glaig,**
  staip

Activity 7. Read the sentences together. Have the student draw a line from the sentence to the picture it matches.

 Jill has a braid in her hair.
 Jack has a pair of socks.
 Ann will get the mail.
 Dad had to paint the den.

Activity 8. Read the words together. Use the alphabet flow-chart to have the student locate the placement of each word under the alphabet letter and then print the words in alphabetical order in the workbook.

 Words: **bait, sail, tail**
  aim, brain, pain
  drain, grain, quail
  aid, bait, rain

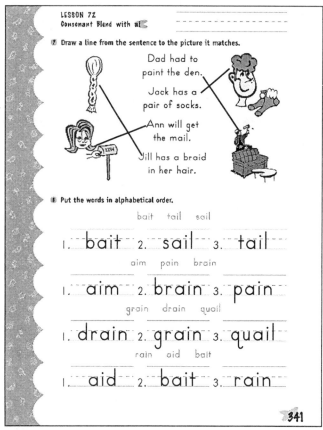

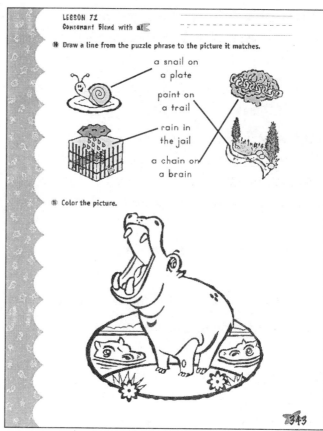

Activity 9. Read the words and sentences together. Discuss the word that would be most appropriate. Have the student print the correct word in the blank.

1. Gail had a (**braid**) in her hair.
2. The dog put his (**tail**) on my leg.
3. The fish had the (**bait**) on his lips.
4. The men will (**sail**) on the lake.
5. The (**train**) will go past the box.
6. Dad ran on the (**trail**) to the lake.

Activity 10. Read the puzzle phrases together. Have the student draw a line from the phrase to the picture it matches.

Pictures: **a snail on a plate**
a chain on a brain
rain in the jail
paint on a trail

Activity 11. Color the picture.

Activity 12. Spell the words under the pictures.

Pictures/Words: **sail, mail, hair**
jail, nail, pain
tail, pail, paid

Horizons Kindergarten Phonics

Lesson 73 - Consonant Blends: pr, tr & Quotation Marks

Overview:

- Review beginning consonant blends
- Introduce beginning consonant blends: **pr**, **tr**
- Introduce quotation marks

Materials and Supplies:

- Teacher's Guide & Student Workbook
- White board
- Reader 2: *Dan Learns to Print*

Teaching Tips:

Review consonant blends used at the beginning of a word. Use the white board to present new beginning consonant blends **pr** and **tr** with both long and short vowels

Introduce quotation marks by verbalizing first. The use of the white board can be effective if a question is asked and the answer is printed with quotation marks around it.

Introduce words: **said, asked, answered** and **yelled.**

Activity 1. Introduce the consonant blend **pr**. Study the pictures and discuss their meaning. Have the student put a circle around each picture that starts with the sound **pr**.

Pictures: **dress, press, prince, print tong, pray, prize, primp**

Activity 2. Practice printing **Pr** and **pr** with capital **P** and lower case **p**.

Activity 3. Introduce the beginning blend **tr**. Study the pictures and discuss their meaning. Have the student put a circle around each picture that starts with the sound **tr**.

Pictures: **trick, track, trash, tack tank, trap, trip, truck**

Activity 4. Practice printing **Tr** and **tr** with capital **T** and lower case **t**.

Activity 5. Study the pictures and discuss their meaning. Have the student circle the letters that make the beginning sound you hear.

Pictures: **pr**ize, **dr**ain, **tr**ack, **cr**ate
print, **tr**ip, **cr**ack, **dr**ip

Activity 6. Introduce quotations and quotation marks. Ask questions and get a responses from the student. Use the white board to print the answer, using quotation marks to indicate the words used in talking. Read the story sentence and emphasize which words are placed between quotation marks. Introduce the words **said**, **asked**, and **answered**. Explore other words that could be used in place of **said**.

> **Dale said, "I went to a big game."**
> **Bob asked, "Did you like the game?"**
> **Dale answered, "It was a good game."**
> **"Can I go with you next time?" asked Bob.**
> **"Yes," said Dale, "I want you to go with me."**

Activity 7. Read the sentences together. Discuss who is talking and where the quotation marks will be placed. Have the student print the sentences on the lines below. Be sure they know which person is talking and where to place the quotation marks.

Dad said, ["]I set the trap.["]
Jim said, ["]Jon ran on the track.["]
["]Can you print the note?["] asked Jane.

Activity 8. Read the words and study the pictures together. Have the student draw a line from the word to the picture it matches.

Pictures: **prong, track, truck, trap, print**

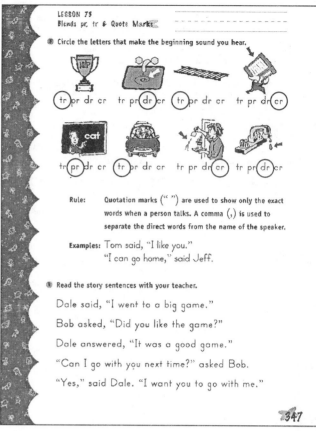

Lesson 74 - Consonant Blends: sl

Overview:

- Review beginning consonant blends
- Introduce beginning consonant blend **sl**
- Creative thinking in making words with specific beginnings and endings

Materials and Supplies:

- Teacher's Guide & Student Workbook
- White board
- Reader 2: *A Ride on a Sled*

Teaching Tips:

Review consonant blends used at the beginning of a word. Use the white board to present the new beginning blend **sl** with both long and short vowels. Discuss various beginning blends and endings of words. Print **cl**, **tr**, **sl** on the board and several endings. Crisscross the parts of words and have the student read them. Encourage the recognition of real words.

Activity 1. Study the pictures and discuss their meaning. Have the student put a circle around each picture that starts with the sound **sl**.

Pictures: **slice, skip, slam, sled
sell, slide, slant, slept**

Activity 2 & 3. Practice printing **Sl** with a capital **S** then with a lower case **s**.

Activity 4. Read the words and discuss their meanings. Have the student draw a line from the word to the picture it matches.

Pictures: **slept, slant, slim, slam, sled**

Activity 5. Read the make-up words.

Make-up Words: **trank, spide, blag, prave**

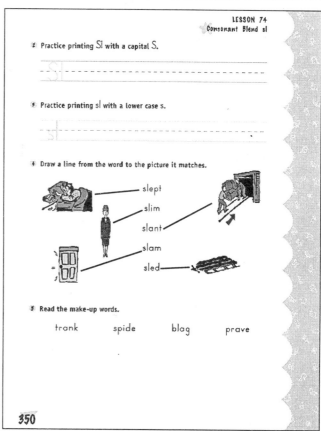

Activity 6. Study the pictures and discuss their meaning. Have the student circle the letters that make the beginning sound you hear.

Pictures: **sk**ip, **sl**ing, **pl**ant, **sk**ull
print, **pr**ay, **cr**ab, **tr**ip

Activity 7. Read the sentences together. Have the student draw a line from the picture to match the sentence.

Pictures: **Ted has a red sled.**
Beth is a slim gal.
Did the cot slant?
Jack has a slot for his mail.

Activity 8. Study the pictures and discuss their meaning. Review beginning blends. Have the student spell the words below the pictures by printing the beginning sounds.

Pictures: **sl**ed, **tr**uck, **cl**ap
crack, **wh**ip, **tr**ap
crutch, **wh**eel, **th**imble
flower, **ch**urch, **sh**oe

Lesson 75 - Consonant Blend: sm

Overview:

- Review beginning consonant blends studied so far
- Introduce beginning consonant blend **sm**
- Alphabetical order

Materials and Supplies:

- Teacher's Guide & Student Workbook
- Alphabet flow-chart
- White board
- Reader 2: *Smell the Roses*

Teaching Tips:

Review consonant blends used at the beginning of a word. Use the white board to present the new beginning blend **sm** with both long and short vowels.

Activity 1. Study the pictures and discuss their meaning. Have the student put a circle around each picture that starts with the sound **sm**.

> Pictures: **smelt, smash, smile, small spell, smoke, grass, smudge**

Activity 2 & 3. Practice printing **Sm** with a capital **S** and then with a lower case **s**.

Activity 4. Read the words together. Study the pictures and discuss the meaning. Introduce the word **Mr**. Have the student draw a line from the word to the picture it matches.

> Pictures: **smock, Mr. Smith, smelt, smell, smash**

Activity 5. Read the words together. Use the alphabet flow-chart to have the student locate the correct placement of each word. The student will print the words in alphabetical order in the workbook.

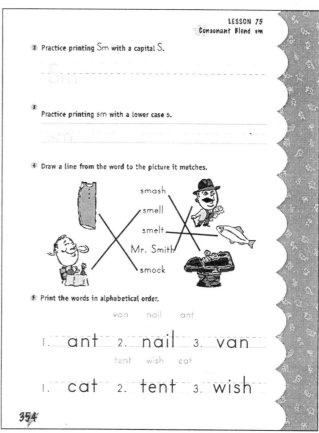

Words: **ant, cat, nail tent, van, wish**

Activity 6. Read the sentences together. Have the student draw a line from the picture to match the sentence. Underline the words that begin with **sm**.

Pictures: **Did Jim smash the van?**
Mr. Smith got a smack on the lips.
A smelt is a fish.
Beth can smell the rose.

Activity 7. Read the words together. Review the rhyming process. Have the student spell the words that rhyme with the first word in the column.

smash/**crash, flash**
smack/**crack, snack**
smog/**fog, log**
smell/**well, spell**

Activity 8. Read the sentence together. Discuss who is talking and where the quotation marks go. Have the student print the sentences and put quotation marks around the talking words.

Mr. Smith said, ["]I can have a snack for lunch.["]
["]I want a smelt for my lunch,["] said Tim.

Activity 9. Study the pictures and discuss the beginning sound. Have the student spell the words below the pictures.

Pictures: **sp**ell, **sm**ell, **sm**oke

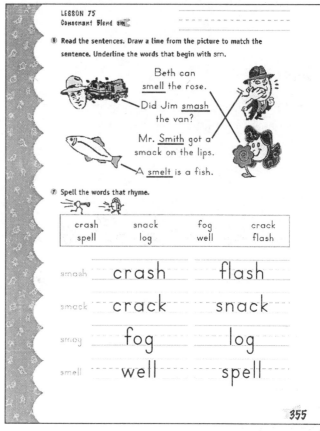

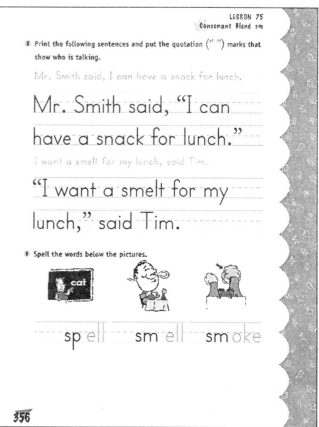

Lesson 76 - Review
Consonant Blend: sn

Overview:

- Review beginning consonant blends studied so far
- Introduce beginning consonant blend **sn**

Materials and Supplies:

- Teacher's Guide & Student Workbook
- White board
- Reader 2: *What Is That Noise?*

Teaching Tips:

Review consonant blends used at the beginning of a word. Use the white board to present the new beginning blend **sn** with both long and short vowels.

Activity 1. Study the pictures and words. Discuss the meaning. Have the students put a circle around each picture that starts with the sound of **sn**.

Pictures: **snap, snack, smack, sniff smile, snip, snug, snag**

Activity 2 & 3. Practice printing **Sn** with a capital **S** then print **sn** with lower-case letters.

Activity 4. Study the pictures and read the words together. Have the student draw a line from the words to the picture it matches.

Pictures: **snack, snag, snip, snap**

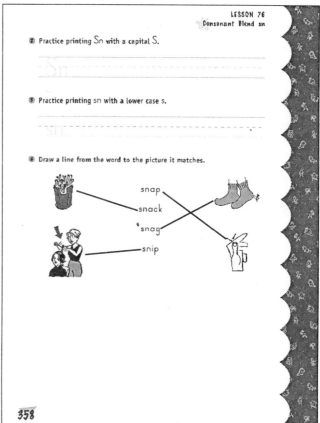

Activity 5. Read the sentences together and discuss the meaning of each. Introduce the sight word saw and my. Have the student draw a line from the picture to the sentence it matches. Underline the words that have **sn** at the beginning.

Pictures: **I had a smelt for my snack.**
It is a snap to slap and clap.
Bill saw a snake in the tent.
Jan is such a snob.

Activity 6. Read the sentences together and study the pictures. Discuss which sentence would be more appropriate to describe each picture. Have the student underline the sentence to match the picture.

The band can snap.
The band can hand.
The tot had a snip for lunch.
The tot had a snack for lunch.
Beth's sock had a snug in it.
Beth's sock had a snag in it.
The bad man had to snatch the mask.
The bad man had to smock the mask.

Activity 7. Read the words together. Review the rhyming process. Have the student spell the words that rhyme with the first one in the column.

snap/**trap, map, flap**
snack/**track, whack, crack**
sag/**wag, rag, tag**
snip/**skip, hip, flip**

Activity 8. Read one word from each of the boxes and have the student put a circle around the correct word in each box.

Words: **snap, smog, stem**
snug, bug, tug
fog, slip, snack
grab, snag, bluff

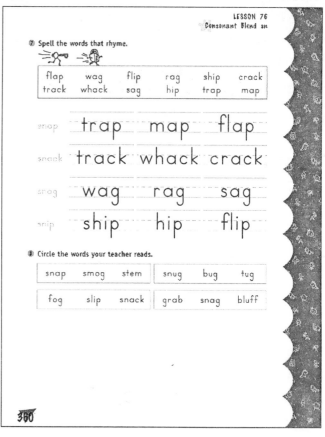

Lesson 77 - Review Consonant Blends and Digraphs

Overview:
- Review consonant blends
- Review consonant digraphs

Material and Supplies:
- Teacher's Guide & Student Workbook
- White board
- Reader 2: *The Fuzzy Runt*

Teaching Tips:

Review all of the consonant blends and digraphs using the white board as necessary.

Activity 1. In the first six activities, the student will review and circle the beginning consonant blend. Have the student and teacher study the pictures together. The student will circle the letters that make the specific sound at the beginning of the word. Review beginning consonant blends: **pr, dr, fl, gr, sn, pl, sm, gl, sl, tr, sp, cl, sk, cr, fr, bl**.

Put a circle around the correct beginning blend.

Pictures: **dr**ip, **gr**ass, **fl**ap, **pr**ank
glad, **sn**atch, **sm**ell, **pl**ant
clap, **tr**ap, **sl**ip, **sp**ell
blast, **cr**ib, **fr**og, **sk**ip

Activity 2. Review beginning consonant blends **sc, br, sn, gr, ch, sh, wh, th**. Put a circle around the beginning blend.

Pictures: **br**ake, **sc**ab, **gr**ade, **sn**ake
thimble, **sh**ed, **wh**ip, **ch**est

Activity 3. Read one word from each of the boxes and have the student put a circle around the correct word in each box.

Words: **think, whisker, ship
crane, drape, flap
blend, brag, clip
grab, glass, spot**

Activity 4. Review consonant **endings**. Read **one** word from each of the lists and have the student put a circle around the **last** sound in the word you read.

Words: 1. **lisp, scat, smell**
2. **sang, skip, plane**
3. **smug, church, snap**
4. **slam, snag, hand**
5. **skull, sent, skid**
6. **sink, slap, fang**
7. **link, class, grade**
8. **disk, flop, drain**
9. **clap, milk, dress**
10. **scalp, camp, prom**

Activity 5. Use some of the endings from the word bank above to make your own make-up words.

Make-up Words: **pra____, spi____
cle____, tro____**

Activity 6. Read the puzzle phrases together. Have the student draw a line from the puzzle phrases to the picture it matches.

Pictures: **a test on a chest
a trap on a hand
a dog with wheels
a cat on skates**

LESSON 77
Review: Blends & Digraphs

Listen to the words your teacher reads. Put a circle around the last sound of the word she or he says.

| sp | ch | nd | nt | ng | nk | sk | mp | lp | lk |

1. lisp   scat   smell   2. sang   skip   plane
3. smug   church snap   4. slam   snag   hand
5. skull   sent   skid   6. sink   slap   fang
7. link   class   grade   8. disk   flop   drain
9. clap   milk   dress   10. scalp   camp   prom

Use some of the endings from the word bank above to make your own make-up words.

pra   spi
cle   tro

363

LESSON 77
Review: Blends & Digraphs

Draw a line from the puzzle phrases to the picture it matches.

a dog with wheels
a cat on skates
a trap on a hand
a test on a chest

364

Lesson 78 – Double Vowels: ea

Overview:

- Review names of vowels used as long vowel sounds
- Introduce double vowel **ea**

Materials and Supplies:

- Teacher's Guide & Student Workbook
- White board
- Reader 2: *A Neat Chain*

Teaching Tips:

Review the Double Vowel Rule: When two vowels are close together in a word, the first one is long (says its own name) and the second one is silent. Use the white board to demonstrate the change from a word with a short vowel to one with a double vowel **ea**. Example: **bed – bead; set – seat; met – meat; best – beast; hat – heat**. Use the technique of crossing out the second vowel and putting a straight line over the first vowel.

Activity 1. Study the pictures and read the words together. Have the student put a circle around those you hear with the long **e** sound.

Pictures: **bean, hear, leaf, dress ear, chain, team, seat**

Activity 2. Study the pictures and read the words together and discuss the meaning. Have the student draw a line from the word to match the picture.

Pictures: **lead, beast, sea, reach**

Activity 3. Study the pictures and read the words together. Have the student print the words that match the pictures. Cross out the second vowel and draw a line over the first one to show that it has a long vowel sound.

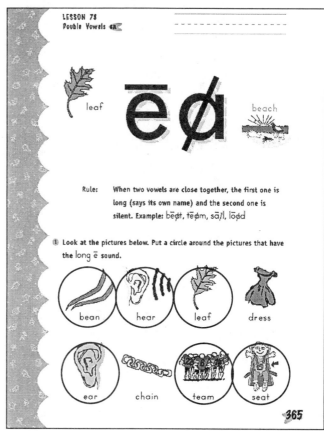

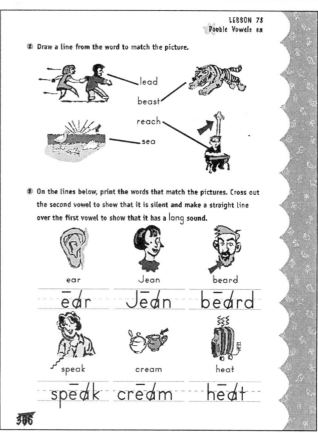

Words/Pictures: **ear, Jean, beard speak, cream, heat**

Activity 4. Read the words together. Review the rhyming process. Have the students spell the words that rhyme with the first one in the column.

ear/**spear, gear, fear**
beam/**dream, cream, team**
real/**deal, veal, heal**
seat/**eat, meat, heat**

Activity 5. Read the sentence with the student. Student will print the sentence on the lines below.

Sentence: **The team can eat the treat.**

Activity 6. Have the students read the make-up words.

Make-up Words: **neaf, teab, reaj, beag**

Activity 7. Read the sentences and words together. Discuss the appropriate word to make the sentence correct. Have the student print the word on the lines below.

1. Jean can sit on the (**beach**).
2. Did you feel the (**heat**) from the fire?
3. I can eat a (**peach**).
4. Dean has a (**bean**) plant.
5. Can you (**teach**) a seal to read?
6. Sam had (**meat**) to eat for his meal.

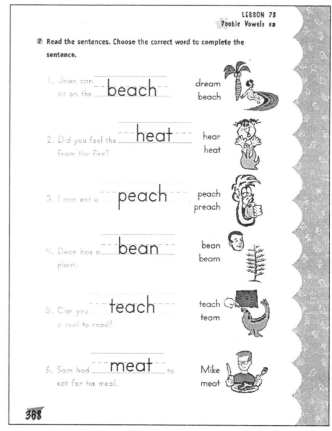

Activity 8. Read the puzzle phrases together. Have the student draw a line from the phrase to the picture it matches.

Pictures: **teach a seat**
Jean on a seal
reach for the beard
a peach can read

Activity 9. Study the pictures together and discuss the spelling words. Have the student practice spelling the words on the white board first by filling in the beginning and ending sound of the word. Then have him spell the words under the pictures in his workbook.

Pictures: **b**ean, **t**each, **s**eat

Activity 10. Have the student practice spelling the words on the white board first by filling in the double vowels in the middle of the word. Then have him spell the words under the pictures in his workbook.

Pictures: **D**ean, sp**ea**k, cr**ea**m
tr**ai**n, m**ai**l, n**ai**l

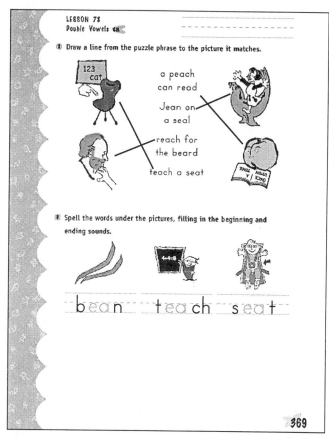

Lesson 79 - Double Vowel: ee

Overview:

- Review long vowels
- Introduce double vowel **ee**

Materials and Supplies:

- Teacher's Guide & Student Workbook
- White board
- Reader 2: *Pee Wee*

Teaching Tips:

Review the sound of the long vowels and the Double Vowel Rule. Use the white board to demonstrate the sound of long **e** as in the word **see**.

Activity 1. Study the pictures and read the words together. Have the student put a circle around those you hear with the long **e** sound.

> Pictures: **beet, weep, pail, sweep bed, creek, three, seed**

Activity 2. Study the pictures and read the words together. Have the student print the words on the lines below. Then he will cross out the second vowel and make a straight line over the first vowel to show that it has a long sound.

> Pictures: **meet, sweep, sheet fleet, greet**

Activity 3. Read the words together and study the pictures. Have the student draw a line from the word to match the picture.

> Pictures: **queen, wheel, weep, seed, meet**

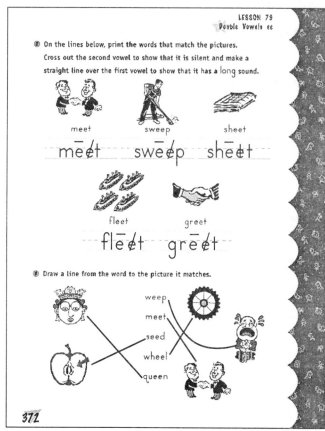

Activity 4. Read the words together. Review the rhyming process. Have the students spell the words that rhyme with the first one in the column.

weep/**jeep, keep, cheep**
seed/**deed, bleed, weed**
sheet/**greet, fleet, sheet**
bee/**see, tee, fee**

Activity 5. Read the make-up words.

Make-up Words: **beeg, deef, meef, teep**

Activity 6. Read the puzzle phrases together. Have the student draw a line from the puzzle phrase to the picture it matches.

Pictures: **feed your feet**
              free a weed
              meet a bee
              a jeep can weep

Activity 7. Read the sentences together and study the pictures. Discuss which sentence would be more appropriate to describe the picture. Have the student underline the sentence to match the picture.

Dee has a bee on her cheek.
Dee has a cheek on her seat.
Teeth can be in a beet.
Dan has teeth.
Take a peek at the seals.
Take a seed at the seals.
Mom made a meal with beef.
Mom made a meal with weep.

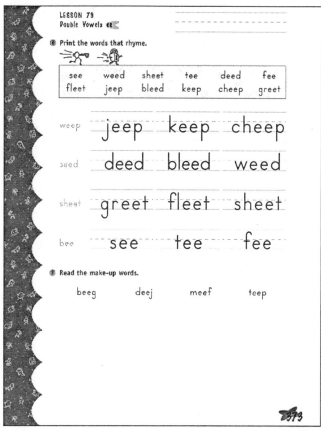

Lesson 80 - Beginning qu & Picture Sequence

Overview:
- Review of beginning blends
- Introduce Letters **qu**
- Introduce picture sequencing

Materials and Supplies:
- Teacher's Guide & Student Workbook
- White board
- Reader 2: *The Quilt*

Teaching Tips:

Explain that the letter **u** always follows **q** and makes the sound we hear at the beginning of **quart**. When the student is beginning to print, be sure to have him begin with the half circle first to avoid confusion with the letter **p**.

With the picture sequencing, allow discussion as to the activity that will follow next. Give several examples verbally.

Activity 1. Study the pictures and words. Discuss the meanings for vocabulary development. Have the student put a circle around each picture that starts with the sound of **qu**.

Pictures: **quack, quench, quick, quill quilt, quit, quiz, quints**

Activity 2 & 3. Practice printing **Qu** with a capital **Q**, then with a lower case **q**.

Activity 4. Study the pictures and read the words together. Discuss the meaning of each. Have the student draw a line from the word to the picture it matches.

Pictures: **quack, quill, quart, quick, quilt**

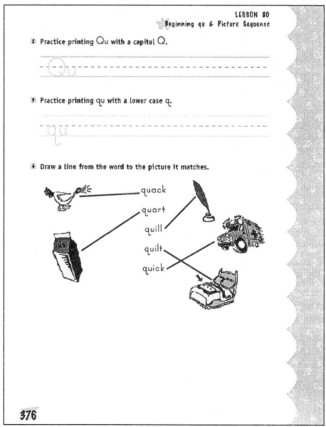

Activity 5. Read the words together. Review the rhyming process. Have the students spell the words that rhyme with the first one in the column.

quack/**back, track, crack**
quit/**flit, kit, slit**
quick/**slick, Dick, flick**
quill/**mill, hill, fill**

Activity 6. Read the sentences together. Have the student draw a line from the picture to match the sentence. Underline the words that begin with **qu**.

Pictures: **I can run, and I am quick.**
Jan has a quilt on her cot.
A duck can quack.
The five kids are quints.

Activity 7. Study the pictures together. Discuss which of the activities would come first in the story. Have the student put a circle around the picture that would come first in the story:

Picture of child getting out of bed in the morning.

Activity 8. Study the third picture that is added to the story. Discuss which picture would come first now. Have the student put a circle around the picture that would come first in the story:

Picture of a mother waking a child up from sleep.

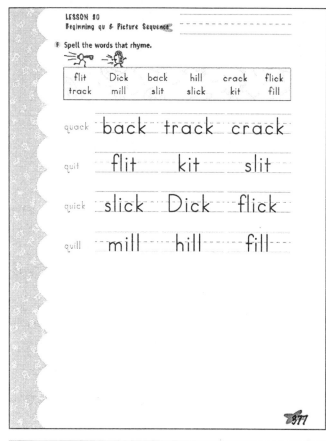

Activity 9. Study the two pictures. Have the student put a circle around the one that would come first in the story:

A man fishing on a river bank.

Activity 10. Study the third picture that is added to the story. Have the student put a circle around the picture that would come first now.

A man taking his rod out of the case and baiting the hook with worms.

Activity 11. Read the sentence. Draw a line under the one that matches the picture.

Jean can fish with bed and wheel.
Jean can fish with a rod and reel.

Activity 12. Spell the words under the pictures by filling in the beginning and ending sounds.

Pictures: **wh**ee**l**, **ch**ee**k**, **d**ee**p**, **b**ee**f**, **m**ee**t**, **s**ee**d**

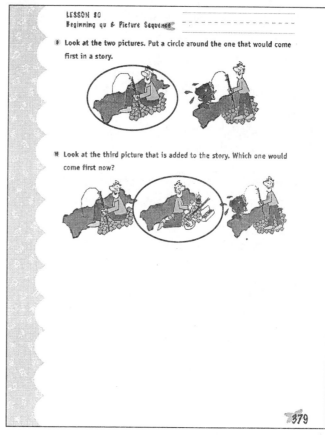